The Search"

SYLVESTER MYSTERIES

D1540319

"The Search is an inter⋯⋯⋯⋯⋯⋯⋯⋯yed
the sharp characterization⋯⋯⋯⋯⋯⋯⋯⋯ It's
nice to see that a mystery novel can be constructed within a
Christian perspective. Good stuff."
— St. Catherines, Ontario

"Heavy on the intrigue, subtle with the theology,
The Search is an enticing distraction."
— *New Man*

"I simply 'crawled behind the haystack' most of Friday
and read *The Search*. I'll probably finish it before closing
my eyes tonight. It's good!"
— Abbotsford, British Columbia

"We both read *The Search* and loved it! We can't wait
until the next one in the series is out."
— Las Vegas, Nevada

SALUSO'S GAME

A BEN SYLVESTER MYSTERY

SALUSO'S GAME

WILLIAM BADKE

MULTNOMAH BOOKS · SISTERS, OREGON

This book is a work of fiction, and all the characters
in this novel are fictional. Any resemblance to actual persons,
living or dead, is purely coincidental.

SALUSO'S GAME

published by Multnomah Books
a part of the Questar publishing family

© 1996 by William Badke
International Standard Book Number: 0-88070-866-2

Cover design by David Uttley
Cover illustration by Tom Collicott
Edited by Rodney L. Morris

Printed in the United States of America

For information:
QUESTAR PUBLISHERS, INC.
POST OFFICE BOX 1720
SISTERS, OREGON 97759

96 97 98 99 00 01 02 03 — 10 9 8 7 6 5 4 3 2 1

So Jacob was left alone, and a man wrestled with him till daybreak. When the man saw that he could not overpower him, he touched the socket of Jacob's hip so that his hip was wrenched as he wrestled with the man.... So Jacob called the place Peniel, saying, "It is because I saw God face to face and yet my life was spared." The sun rose above him as he passed Peniel, and he was limping because of his hip.

GENESIS 32:24-25, 30-31

T he rebel troops started firing as soon as the chopper lifted off, aiming for the rotor and the engine, bullets winging everywhere. Blasting away in their fear, watching their last chance at life disappearing into the sky, who could blame them for wanting to destroy us.

It was chaos inside the chopper. Karen sheltered the kids as best she could while bullets ripped through the fuselage all around us. The chopper dipped and veered to the left while the bullets followed it. A steep climb, then a bank to the right and it looked like we were winning, moving out of range, but then the engine started to sputter.

Karen looked across from where she sat, terror on her face, as the chopper plunged, falling toward the jungle, and there was nothing I could do. They were screaming as the chopper dropped and crashed and I was shouting but I couldn't help them.

"Ben." Someone was shaking me. "Ben, wake up."

"What?"

"It's not real, Ben. Not real. It's another dream." Karen. I was home in my bed and the whole thing had been a trick of the mind, not real. Only I knew that every part of the dream was true, everything had actually happened just as I pictured it, and the fact that Karen was alive beside me now was just one more miracle along the way.

"My leg's hurting like crazy," I said.

"Take a pill. Please, Ben."

"I'm too dependent on them already."

"You know the dreams are bound to stop sometime," she said, holding me close. "Why don't you try to sleep?"

But I couldn't sleep. My mind was filled with the chopper falling from the sky. I hadn't been able to help her and it was my fault Karen nearly died.

The whole thing had started with that meeting with Simpson. I should have been tougher on him. I should have told him to find some other sucker for a mission as risky as the one he was trying to talk me into. Who cares that it was a board decision?

Simpson, chief of operations, had planned the meeting with me carefully—a written memo a week before, two reminders after that. He'd worn a dark blue blazer with a power tie and carried an impressive stack of paper under his arm.

Right at one o'clock that afternoon he'd knocked on the door of my office, and when I let him in I could see that he'd brought his whole dog and pony show with him—file folders, maps, and his assistant Darren, who never contributed anything to these meetings but added to the solemnity of the occasion.

"New assignment?" I asked, sitting down behind my desk and motioning them into the chairs I'd set out. Simpson only smiled. He sat down carefully and laid out the files and maps on my desk. Darren stared at the wall above my head.

"Where to?" I asked.

"Africa," Simpson told me. "How's your comfort zone?"

"With Africa? Nobody ever gets comfortable with Africa."

"Can you be operational in an African setting?" Simpson always sounded like a twenty-year man in CIA administration.

"I'll be okay," I told him.

"His name is Saluso. Governor of a state in the country of Mtobe. That's West Africa."

"Mtobe's a democratic country," I objected. "What does this Saluso want from us?"

"He had some difficulties when he ran for president a few months ago."

"Well it should be obvious to you by now that I'm not very good at hand-holding," I said.

"It's nothing like that. He's requested tactical support for his next electoral opportunity," Simpson said, not hesitating a microsecond over any of the big words he'd used.

"Come on, Simpson. I'm not into PR."

"There's good reason to believe that a Saluso election victory would be good for the free world."

"You've obviously forgotten the business we're in," I said. "Our company is named Libertec. Lib-er-tec. We go to *non*-democratic situations and help democratic movements succeed. I'm a political advisor, not a spin-doctor or campaign manager."

"Don't be facetious, Ben," Simpson said. "There are certain facts about this assignment that have to remain under wraps. Trust me that this thing is within our mandate."

"Those of us who are humble slaves of Libertec have work to do," I told him. "Don't forget to shut the door on your way out."

He stared at me for a second, probably wondering about the wisdom of doing away with corporate hierarchies. "Don't you want to hear about Saluso?" he asked.

"Not particularly. I've got another job coming up in a week and I don't have time to take this one anyway."

"We'll reschedule the other one. Listen to me, Ben. You have to understand about Saluso."

I gave up. Simpson was a legend for his stubbornness, so I put my elbows on the desk and dropped my face into my hands. "Shoot," I said.

"He started his career as a physicist," Simpson went on, "but grassroots involvements pushed him into the governorship. When he ran for president, someone accused him of planning to cheat, and they ended up mounting a UN supervisory team to monitor the vote. Saluso lost badly."

"Was he crooked?"

"Our best intelligence says not." Every time Simpson used the word *intelligence,* I thought "oxymoron."

"Don't tell me about your intelligence, Simpson," I said, rolling up my sleeve to show him once again the scar on my arm.

"This is getting old, Ben," he said.

"The reason I have this scar, Simpson, is that someone in

Libertec leaked my whereabouts to some very bad people who in turn—"

"Give it up, Ben."

"—who in turn hired a really big bad guy to stab me. How's your progress on finding out who's the weasel in Libertec?"

"There is no weasel and your paranoia has nothing to do with Saluso."

"It has everything to do with my safety and whether I'm about to be hung out to dry one more time. What does this African want from me anyway?"

"Advice about mounting a presidential campaign that's above reproach. He wants an absolutely clean run at the presidency next time."

"He's got what—three-and-a-half years before the next election?"

"Approximately."

"So he's already put on a dirty campaign and he has three years to cool his heels before he can try again. What's to say he's not planning a coup?"

"You're not a particularly trusting person, are you?" Simpson said. Darren was still staring at the wall.

"He smells bad. I don't want to do this."

"The assignment comes from the highest levels, Ben."

My heart dropped. This was a board level operation, and I was the sacrificial lamb. No objections allowed.

"I'll run it by Karen and let you know tomorrow," I said. "Don't forget to close the door." Kicking Simpson out of my office was the only satisfaction I was going to get out of the afternoon.

When I told Karen about it that night, I hoped she'd get the same bad vibes I did. But she didn't share my doubts. From her perspective, it was the perfect solution for a husband who'd been riding a desk too long and was getting grouchy at home. She gave me her blessing.

About nine o'clock that night, the phone rang. Karen answered and passed it over to me.

"Hey, Ben. How you doing?" A voice I didn't recognize.

"Sorry," I said, "who's calling?"

"Sid. Sid Murphy."

"I don't know any Sid Murphy."

"College. Thought I'd made a stronger impression on you."

Sid. Sure, nonconformist Sid Murphy. I found it coming back quickly. He was older than the rest of us—big dreams but no personal discipline. Most of us expected him to end up as some South Seas beach bum.

"Where you calling from?" I asked.

"Africa. Mtobe. From what I hear, you're planning to visit us."

"Who told you something like that, Sid?"

"Governor Saluso and I know each other. I hear you got your masters degree and now you're some sort of international political advisor."

"We work with democratic movements," I said.

"Too bad I never made it past a B.A. Sounds like quite the job. In fact, you'd be a perfect fit for Saluso. You think you could help him, get him on the right track?"

"If I was willing to take the job."

"Look, you married? Kids?"

"One wife, two kids."

"How'd you like a first-class all expenses paid vacation for four in a top of the line beach hotel. My hotel." I could sense the boasting in his voice.

"It's not the way we do things, Sid. For the most part I leave my family at home when I'm on a job."

"You're free to check it out, Ben. If you like, I'll send you a couple of brochures. Two weeks totally on the house is nothing to sneeze at."

"What's the catch?"

"I'll be up front about this, okay? A little birdie told me you needed some incentive to do a very important job for a very deserving African governor."

I should have seen it right away. I should have gone to the board and told them that Libertec had lots of stupider employees who'd be delighted to go in my place.

That's what I should have done.

CHAPTER ONE

BEN

The note of the engines changed, and I felt the familiar chill of descending into another unknown world as the plane banked and the rumble of high flight turned into the roar of landing. Ahead was the tedious dance of customs and immigration and health check and currency check—everything designed like a spider web for the unwary. I'd done it often enough, but every time was a new experiment in suspense.

Even then, when it was too late to do anything about it, I wondered how I could have been such a fool, bringing my family with me on the vague promise of a one-time friend who claimed to own a luxury hotel on the beach. It made no sense. But Karen was the one who wanted an adventure. She was trying out her wings now that she'd discovered she didn't need to hide in my shadow anymore. I could hardly begrudge her the chance, after the botch I'd made of our lives a few months before.

Jack stirred beside me, his seven-year-old head heating my arm as he slept. Jimmie was across the aisle with Karen, always with Karen. But life had been good in the past few months, and we were becoming whole again.

All of us still endured the disturbing memories of the past year. It was me who struggled most with it, remembering the mistakes I'd made, one of which maybe got an ally killed. I'd almost put my whole family in the grave with my stupidity.

"Dad?"

"It's okay, Jack. We're almost there." I looked into his eyes, now wide open, and was stunned that he was becoming a person all his own. His brown eyes and dark hair gave him a maturity beyond his years. I could pride myself that I was even starting to connect with him and Jimmie.

I began filling out our declaration forms. Average family, unusual vacation. Mtobe was not a typical tourist destination. I call it "Mtobe" because Libertec wants nothing in print about the location of its clients. If you can guess where we were, then bully for you, but none of the names you will see except those of my family are genuine. Think West Africa, jungle, bugs, snakes, friendly people—most of them.

"Have you got the forms, Ben?" Karen's eyes connected with mine across the aisle, and again I was struck by the clarity on her face, the freshness, as if she were newly made and undamaged by the tribulations that turn the rest of us into carping whiners.

"Working on them," I murmured, filling out the details I would need to go over again verbally once we reached the ground. One thing that every Third World civil servant could bless colonialism for was the stunningly complex bureaucracy it left behind. Nothing could be done with less than four copies, twenty-seven signatures and fifty-three rubber stamps.

"You scared, Dad?"

"Not really. How about you?"

"Nope." Jack's bravado was thin.

"I hear there's great swimming right outside the hotel," I told him.

"Are there any sharks?"

"Shark meeting a tough guy like you would turn tail and run. Take all his friends with him too."

The change in me was startling. I could feel it in my relationships, like a destroying wound was healing leaving only a small scar. I still thought about it often—the chilling moment when I realized that Karen had been kidnapped, my botched attempt to rescue her, the people who died, the emptiness at the end of it even though I had my family back safe and sound.

We came in for the final run, the tarmac and surrounding fields a scar in the jungle. Beyond was the city, then the coast, a line of sand clearly visible except where the river washed out through clumps of mangrove.

"Are you buckled?" I asked Jack

"Sure, Dad."

Strange, the feeling I was starting to have for him and for scrappy little Jimmie. Like being reborn. I looked at Karen. She was tightening Jimmie's belt—he tended to squirm.

We landed, the tropical air bouncing us all the way down, with me imagining an air pocket that stretched to ground zero, smacking us down like a pancake tossed on a griddle. Then we were rolling in, and I relaxed, unhooking my fingers from the armrest. So I'm not a good traveler. Some people are that way.

Getting off was the usual mob scene—passengers stumbling over each other, too much hand luggage making everything awkward, the humidity on the tarmac hitting us like a warm wet towel. I took Karen's hand, two bags slung over my other shoulder, the kids grabbing whatever they could of us.

"Keep close, Ben," Karen said as we walked toward the terminal, and I sensed a bit of the insecurity she'd grown up with.

"Piece of cake," I said.

"When do we get to the beach, Dad?" Jimmie hadn't slowed at all since we started. Maybe that's why Karen was looking so worn.

Then, bursting toward us out of the shade of the terminal, I saw a swarm of at least fifteen young African males pushing each other in their eagerness to get to the passengers. Trouble.

"Carry your cases?" one of them shouted, his voice young, harsh.

"I see them first!" bellowed another. They swarmed us, a crush of teenagers obviously unofficial and likely dangerous, dressed in rags, some of them leprous, all of them eager to carry our luggage for a fee or trample us if we resisted them.

"Ben!" Karen shouted, dragging our kids in close, both of us struggling to hold our bags as fingers grabbed at them. Faces thrust themselves at us from every direction, loud voices.

"You," I said, seizing the arm of the guy who looked least likely to hurt us. The others moved in on the rest of the passengers, and we let the guy, dressed in bizarre stripes and slashes, carry our bags to the customs check-in. I paid him too much.

Once inside the terminal building, we regrouped. "Everyone okay?"

"What was that all about?" Karen asked. "We haven't even cleared customs."

"Airport rats. In some countries they've pretty well taken over."

"Are we safe in here?"

"I thought we'd be safe out there. Who knows? You're the one longing for an adventure."

"Those guys were crazy, Dad." Jack was fully traumatized.

"Are they going to come in here?" asked my youngest.

"No, Jimmie." I looked around at the terminal—a warehouse with bedlam thrown in. Suitcases were on a manual conveyor, and we dug ours out. Somewhere in the building there must have been air conditioning, but this wasn't it. I was beginning to feel that familiar tropical clamminess—damp clothes on damp skin, sweat dripping through my eyebrows to blur my vision.

"Where do we go now?" Karen looked confused by the noise. The kids were clinging close.

"Let's not panic. We'll be funneled through about four checkpoints. I've got all the papers, so follow my lead and do what they tell you to do. Don't argue. Don't answer them any more than they ask."

Karen gave me a look, a combination of excitement, anxiety, and exhaustion. "I feel really strange, Ben. There's going to be trouble."

"Not if I can help it," I said.

We made it through passport and visa control, the immigration officer pausing about as long as I expected considering his mission to leave the public quaking in their boots. At the customs inspection desk, they searched our bags with the precision of a surgeon hunting for cancer cells but sent us on. Health control was a breeze if you ignore the ten minutes of questioning they put us through.

"We're almost there," I said. "One more to go."

Even though I had the currency form filled out perfectly, it was clear that the fourth official wasn't in the same league as the others. His uniform was just that much crisper, and he wore dark glasses. What was more, he'd gathered a big line in front of him.

"How were you getting such a lot of Mtobe currency?" This to the woman in front of us, American, not used to taking guff.

"Money exchange in the States. I had to go to five of them to get this much," she said.

"You are ordered to enter the country with foreign currency. Where is your authorization to have this?"

"Come on," she said. "I bought the money on the open market. You guys really have your nerve squeezing us for our currency because yours won't buy anything outside Mtobe."

The official must have been mellowing. He grinned and said, "If you had been my wife, I would slap your face."

She turned icily cooperative after that and got through in minutes.

"You are holding currency for your family?" This to me.

"Yes."

"Wife and children have none?"

"We'll share later." I shouldn't have said it.

He frowned, staring at the form. "Let me view your currency, and your credit cards if you have such."

I got out the traveler's checks. He counted them, frowning more, then fingered my cards.

"This is not in order."

"Excuse me?"

He turned to Karen. "You are free," he said. Then back to me. "Come with me, please."

"What's the problem?" I asked him.

Karen's face had gone chalky. "Where are you taking my husband?" she asked, her voice pitched high.

"Don't worry, Karen," I said as the man put his fingers around my arm. "Wait with the kids over there."

"Wherever we're going it's got to be together. All four of us together."

"Madam." The official's face was tense. "I said that you are free. There is a large room through those doors where you are permitted to wait."

"But—"

"Don't, Karen," I said, my eyes warning her. "Just stay in the airport, and I'll join you soon."

She gave in then, but as I turned to follow the currency official, I saw her making a praying hands sign. We went into a sparse office—just a desk and two hard chairs.

One man sat there, black, sixtyish, gray at the temples, suit and tie. He rose. "I am sorry—sorry, Mr. Sylvester. There has been no other way." He made a motion of dismissal to the currency official, who left quickly without looking at me.

"Way for what? You're frightening my family and you know my currency is in order. What's the problem?"

"This is not about currency."

I waited. Obviously someone had set up the agenda and had forgotten to share it with me. The silence quickly became deafening.

"Do you have no questions, Mr. Sylvester?"

"None worth asking."

"Clearly you will not frighten easily."

"Look," I said, "my family's out there in the lobby, scared to death. That makes whatever you're doing here something less than a game. Are you looking for a bribe?"

"Please. Nothing like that. I am too sorry about your family. They are safe."

"Who do you represent?"

"Governor Saluso."

I got up and walked to the door. "Tell him I'll see him in a couple of days. It's all arranged. There's no need for this." How did I know that when I turned the handle it would be locked?

"Please stay for a time, Mr. Sylvester. Rest yourself." The man's voice was deep, almost hypnotizing, his accent a mixture of native language and cultured British. He seemed out of place in this sparse office, as if he would normally be found in a large room with plush carpets, significant paintings on the walls.

"There's no need for this," I repeated.

"I believe that there is a need. May I tell you a brief story?"

"Do I have a choice?"

"Once, Mr. Sylvester," he went on, "once there was a ruler. Shall we call him Kunji?"

"Why not?" I said.

"He was not the supreme ruler, although he should have been. Indeed, he had risen to the governance of a small territory within the land. But he wanted to do more. One day he determined to enter the national election and take his rightful post at the head of the nation."

"But he lost the election because he cheated," I put in. "It left him bitter, so he hatched a plot to take the nation by force."

The man looked surprised. "Who has been telling you such a thing?"

"I work for a company that makes it a priority to avoid being embarrassed."

"Mr. Sylvester..." I waited. He seemed about to become apologetic. For my part, I was battling the old anger that snarled whenever someone got pushy.

"Mr. Sylvester," he began again. "I am not accustomed to dealings like this, please believe me. If there had been another path to walk, I would be walking in it, but I am a man under orders."

"Why do I suspect that you're about to do something nasty?"

"We are not barbarians here." He pushed an intercom button, and a second later Sid Murphy walked in.

"Hey, Ben." He'd aged. Maybe it was the tropics, but the

scraggly gray hair, the deep lines around the eyes, spoke of tribulation or suffering or something. There was also that familiar sly dog look about him that I remembered so well. Sid Murphy, my old college acquaintance, in the flesh, here in Mtobe.

"The plan was for us to go to your hotel, Sid," I said. "You didn't need to come to the airport."

"Sure I did. There's a bunch of people who wouldn't be pleased if they heard you were here."

"Looks to me like everyone's gone out of his way to roll out the welcome mat. Who else gets dragged into a small office and interrogated before he's even passed currency control?"

"Listen to me, Ben. The governor of the state you're going to—"

"Saluso."

"Governor Saluso. From what I understand, he called your company in to help him gear up for the next election."

"And we told him," I said, "that he needed PR people, not political advisors. Did he explain it to you?"

"Some. He insisted that your people were the kind he needed. And he could pay."

"We're very choosy, Sid. I'm amazed my company even gave him the time of day, to tell the truth. Then when I got a call from an old acquaintance—"

"Friend."

"—friend inviting the whole family to your resort, I figured you must work for Saluso on the side. Still, we appreciate the free family vacation."

"You've got work to do first."

"So give me a chance to get Karen and the kids settled. Saluso can send a car for me."

"Ben. I'll get your family settled, and this man here will sneak you in to Saluso."

"Why?"

"Can't take the risk of someone hijacking you before you get to do the job."

"Hijacking? What is this?"

"Just do what we tell you, Ben. It's for your safety."

"Can I say good-bye to my family?" I asked.

"Write a note."

"Come on, Sid."

He handed me a piece of paper. I had my own pen. It took some thinking. I mean, I could have reassured her and maybe sent her off happy, but she deserved to know. These people had enough power to bribe a federal currency inspector into letting me be snatched, so I knew they held all the cards for the time being.

Karen could pray. As far as I knew I was about to become a nonperson. Snakes were loose and I was the prey.

So I wrote the note:

Karen—

Slight change in plans. Sid promises me he'll look after you, and I'll see you maybe by Saturday. Don't worry—I'm not sorry I brought you and the kids. In fact, if we'd brought the cat, we'd have the whole household basking in the tropics.

Love,
Ben

I folded the note and smiled at Sid. "Take care of them or I'll have your head."

I turned to the African and said stupidly, "I'm ready. Take me to your leader."

For someone whose mind was growing numb, I thought I was doing pretty well.

CHAPTER TWO

KAREN

aren watched the official lead Ben away. She made a praying hands sign and saw her husband flash her an awkward smile. Then he was gone.

The public waiting room where the official had told her and the children to wait was air-conditioned and modern—so civilized she could have believed Ben would be gone only for a few minutes, an hour at most. Just some formality that Ben with his witty charm could quickly straighten out. She couldn't bear the thought of having to wait any more than an hour.

But she'd seen the look he'd given her, and she knew the problem was far more serious than that. Neither of them were ready for trouble like this, especially not after the events of the past year. That's why she felt her panic rising, and she had to breathe deeply to slow down her heart. They might be torturing him, and she couldn't do anything about it. What was more, she had the kids to look after, in a strange country, with no money and no one to meet her.

She blamed herself for agreeing so easily to the trip after

they got the phone call from Sid Murphy. It was hard for her to resist the thought of a free vacation on the beach in an exotic African country. But that was only the beginning of her reasons. The main motivation was Ben. He was taking the first baby steps on his most important journey, and she wanted him near her.

For twenty minutes she waited in an airport in a strange country with two children who were done sitting still, and the only thing she could do to help was pray.

"Mom, what if he doesn't come back?" Jack, her thinker, her worrier. She and Ben were going to have cause to regret that God had blessed their oldest son with such a wild imagination.

"He'll be back real soon. Have you ever known your dad to let us down?"

"Then why are you praying?" he asked.

"I pray a lot lately. God wants us to tell him when we've got a problem."

"Is Dad being a problem?" Jimmie asked. He was still too young to grasp a lot of complexities, but it saved him from the worries of his parents.

"No one's being a problem. When Dad comes back, we'll go to the hotel."

That's when Sid Murphy came into the room—a thin, scruffy looking man in jeans and a T-shirt with yellow flowers on it. Karen knew from her first sight of him that the man was capable of almost any kind of evil. She could read all over him that he had the power to hurt them badly.

"Mrs. Sylvester?" he said. "I'm Sid Murphy. Look, I know this is a change in plans for you, but Ben's got to get to the state capital quickly. He asked me to give you this."

The note he held out to her in his sun-wrinkled hand was exactly what she feared it would be—short and upbeat, until she read the part about their cat that didn't exist.

She'd grown up in the home of the owner of a large electronics company, and she learned very early that people with influence generally got what they wanted. As a child, she had power all around her, available for her use whenever she needed it. Now she had nothing to defend her family with. What difference would it have made if she'd called the embassy? The only evidence she had that anything was wrong was a jaunty little note from her husband.

It was tempting to confront Sid Murphy right then and there, but she decided not to take the risk. She felt like a fly caught in a spider's web—the more it struggles the more snarled up it gets. This trip wasn't supposed to be a big tribulation. "We were supposed to be resting from all the terrors of this past year," she told God, there in the waiting room. "God, we were supposed to be resting."

She wondered at how quickly her mind turned to blaming God. If truth be told, she probably would have been dead a long time ago if it hadn't been for him. But there in that big room, looking up from Ben's note into the face of Sid, it was all she could do to pretend that everything was fine or that God still had everything under control.

"What is it, Mom?" Jack asked.

"It's okay. Dad had to meet the people from the government early. We knew he'd be away for awhile, but he's coming to meet us Saturday."

"Yeah, right."

"Don't make a fuss, kids. Everything's fine."

"There's a car waiting to take you to the hotel," Murphy said. "My driver will carry your bags." He snapped his fingers, and a tall black man came toward them from a corner of the room.

The car was a Mercedes limo, dark blue and shiny. Once all of them were inside and the car started moving, the boys kept themselves amused by taking in the scenery. The landscape was dominated by the color green, the palm trees and the undergrowth so thick someone could get lost in it ten feet away and never be found. It would have been a sauna for them by then except for the air conditioning. She found it amazing that so many people went about their lives as if the heat and humidity meant nothing.

They saw all the dirt and squalor while they rode in cool comfort in their Mercedes on the way to a luxury hotel on the beach. Karen wondered how anyone in good conscience could reconcile the difference. The people looked cheerful, loud, and hopeful, but she knew that deep suffering must be eating into every day of their lives. Suffering was something she was coming to understand.

Fear for Ben filled her mind. The wheels had come off their dream vacation but no one had told her why. Where had they taken him?

She remembered the time before Mtobe, the time Ben had trouble talking about. She remembered the depression that had almost consumed him after her kidnapping and the fire and the people who died. It frustrated her that he couldn't talk about it, couldn't express the words, that he was trying to be tough and take charge while inside he was shriveling up.

One night he woke her, and in the darkness he told her he couldn't go on. He told her he felt as if he were dying.

Karen understood that he'd been struggling all his life for a corner of his own, the ability to do what he had to do without anyone blocking his way, telling him that he wasn't smart enough, strong enough. And then he had started the fire.

"It's guilt that's eating you, Ben," she said to him that night, but he told her it was more than guilt. It was loneliness, as if he'd been locked in a back room where he could hear and see everything but couldn't communicate with anyone.

"Jesus died, he shed his blood to pay for everything you've ever done. And he's alive now. He can make all the difference," she said. But he told her that some things could never be forgiven. And so she explained it all to him, the whole story, and for the first time he grasped the reality that God had not made him for loneliness or night terrors or those dreams that ate him up.

"All you have to do, Ben, is give him your life."

"Only my life?" he said, knowing that if he did what she was saying, God would take his corner away, the control, the power of not being too weak. She was asking too much, but he knew it was true. He'd seen the change in her.

So he lay back in bed and looked at the dark ceiling and said, "Yes. I can't live like this. You can have my life, Jesus, you can do what you want. You can forgive me and change me and I'll let you have the whole thing, such as it is."

Not a very glamorous start to the journey.

So Karen sat on the same seat as Sid Murphy in his rough blue jeans and sissy shirt with the bold yellow flowers, keeping her distance from him, while her kids sat on the seat facing them because they'd never ridden backwards in a car before, and she savored the memory of Ben's claw-like grasp at faith in a resurrected Lord.

As they moved out of the city, the traffic gradually changed from cars and trucks to the pedestrians, goats, and chickens of the countryside. The kids were enthralled with the sights. There were school kids in uniforms, many carrying banana leaves over their heads to keep off the rain. Bicycles carried everything—from four people to a basket seller whose goods were strapped to him, making him almost as big as a compact car.

Karen found she couldn't stop glancing at Sid Murphy. He was in his middle fifties, but he looked as though he'd lived at least another decade, his face wrinkled and his skin leathery. Even if he'd worn a business suit, he would have seemed scraggly to her. She saw greed and cruelty in his eyes, all masked with a pleasant little grin, as if he wanted everyone to be his friend. She wondered how Ben could ever have called someone like that a friend, or even admitted he knew him.

"You'll love the hotel," Sid said. He said it to her as if nothing was wrong, as if Ben was really going to be back with them all smiles on Saturday.

"Will I?" she asked.

"Ben will be fine, believe me. The last thing he told me was to make sure you really got a vacation. He figured all of you would have a week together as a family after he got back."

"I wish I could believe you." She knew her voice was flat, but she couldn't hide the defeat she felt. They'd been through so much, and she had no strength to do anything but fear the worst.

None of this was fair as far as she could see. She'd been faithful to God. She'd led her husband to God. Was it going to be the same endless round of pain for the rest of their earthly existence? In her mind, she imagined God telling her family, "Measure out the amount of trouble you think you can bear." When they had it all measured into a bowl, he took a ladle and added five or six more scoops.

She wasn't rebellious or even angry with him yet, just questioning, just wondering why their lives were like a complicated game where only God knew the rules.

To add to the mix of things, their driver was constantly honking the horn just like every other driver; it sounded like an automotive version of a John Cage symphony. Africa promised to be the noisiest place she'd ever visited.

She couldn't stop thinking about Ben. Was he all right? How could he be all right? How could she help him? Her thoughts were flitting all over the place while she prayed and tried to hold back the dread that kept rising up in her chest. She wondered how any of this could be fair.

Then something hammered into the window and left a big pock mark in the glass only inches from her face. The driver swerved hard, and something started banging up and down the car while more pock marks splattered all over the glass she'd just been looking through. The car rocked with the concussions of something violent hitting them again and again.

The driver flung the car into a series of S-curves, and she dragged Jack and Jimmie to the floor and threw herself on top of them, terror rising as she realized that someone was shooting at them and those were real bullets hitting the car.

Make it stop, her mind started pleading. Make it stop. Save us.

The kids were silent underneath her while the car swerved and braked and accelerated and tossed them back and forth, but Karen managed to keep them under her. All the while the hammering went on and on. She realized suddenly that she was going to be sick.

Then there was only silence, and the car was still moving, the attack over as suddenly as it had begun.

"Jack! Jimmie!"

"I'm okay, Mom," Jack said. "Get off me." Jimmie was whimpering, unable to understand what had happened. She reached down for him as she struggled back up onto the seat, and he came into her arms, crying but not hurt. The windows were full of marks, but they weren't broken.

"The car's armored," Sid Murphy explained to her, his face intense and angry.

She could imagine what Ben would have said to him then—"Got some enemies, Sid? I'd appreciate it if you made friends with them before you ask my family to ride in your toy with you"—but she was too shaken to say anything.

Sid leaned forward and said to Jack, "Did you see anyone?"

"No," Jack said. He seemed to share Karen's impression of Sid Murphy.

"Either of you see anything?" he asked Jimmie and Karen.

"No," she said. Jimmie had no interest in talking. Karen buckled him in beside her, searching in her mind for the right words. Then she screwed up her courage and just asked it. "Sid, were those people shooting at you or at us?"

"I've got some unfriendly acquaintances," he muttered. "That's why the car is bullet-proofed."

"I don't think you really answered my question."

"Look, Mrs. Sylvester, why don't we go back and ask those people with the machine guns. They're bound to tell us who they're working for."

"Are we in danger?"

"I don't think so. Honest. I wouldn't have brought you with me if I did."

"Is Ben in danger?"

Instead of answering, he turned his face away from her and stared out the window. Karen gave up trying to talk to him. Both kids were quiet.

Her first sight of the hotel—as fantastic as she expected it to be—left her feeling cold. The hotel was right on the beach, five stories in a peach color, ringed with palm trees. Carpet on the floor, chandelier in the lobby, a terrific suite big enough for eight.

She let the kids swim in the pool while she sat on the edge, her feet resting in the water, an endless prayer on her lips.

CHAPTER THREE

BEN

I was in hell as we whispered down the highway. "It's air-conditioned, Mr. Sylvester," the man had told me. Only something shut down along the way, and I was in the trunk of a limo in the tropics with only five or six air holes to the underside of the car, and no air conditioning. Even to get the holes open, I had to force aside a cover. The carbon monoxide was at least 50-50 with the oxygen.

Earlier, Saluso's man had led me out of the terminal by a back door, and the limousine waiting for us was about what I expected from someone like Saluso. But when the driver opened the trunk and casually gestured for me to get in, I balked.

"This is, of course, not a normal proceeding, Mr. Sylvester," Saluso's man admitted while the driver stood there looking frustrated. He said it as if he explained such things on a daily basis. "We understand your doubt, but the compartment is large, and you have a light plus the finest of air conditionings."

Then everything died after five minutes of driving, and I was left in the dark with a suddenly vanishing air supply. Panicked, I fumbled around for something, anything that would open and give me oxygen, but the trunk I was lying in was built like a storage locker in a Sherman tank.

Just when I thought I was about to check out for good, I found a removable cover over some airholes they must have drilled as a backup. By then, even undoing the hand-tightened knobs was almost beyond me. Wrenching hard, I pulled the cover aside and put my mouth right over one of the holes, sucking air.

Once I could breathe a bit, I started banging on things. Nobody paid any attention. I couldn't help thinking how my bosses back at the home office in Seattle would have been enraged at people treating their expensive property so shabbily. Or maybe not—we hadn't been on the best of terms lately.

All the while, Karen and the kids were a burden on the edge of my thoughts. In the hands of Sid Murphy, they were probably just being kept out of the way. But they could be used for leverage if I didn't cooperate with whatever was going down.

Dark. Dark and hot, with only the dim light of the air holes, and I found myself praying as if I'd done it all my life. This was a perfect time to put my fledgling faith to the test, but I would have preferred not to take the exam, especially when I didn't know how long I'd be there or whether or not the carbon monoxide would get me before we got to wherever it was we were going.

Finally, after I'd endured a couple of hours or more of

semi-suffocation, we turned off the main road, the car pulled to a stop, and eventually the trunk flipped open. When he saw me, the guy who put me in there—I never did learn his name, Saluso's man from the office at the airport—didn't exactly say "whew," but his face showed it. I needed a shower and fast. Every inch of me was soaked.

I crawled out of the trunk—joints screaming at me, the sweat burning my eyes, anger burning in my chest—and took several deep breaths. Some water would have done nicely.

We were in a courtyard ringed with a concrete wall eight feet high, broken glass set in the top of it. One building dominated—a large house or small hotel, take your pick, made out of concrete molded in curves and swirls, painted pale green. There were two or three outbuildings, but everything focused on the big one, Saluso's palace.

I was having trouble walking, my knees like pudding. Saluso's man had to help me to the veranda of the house. When he'd left me on the stairs, he knocked on the door, muttered something to whoever opened it, then went back to his limo and shouted at the driver to get going. I never saw him again. Someone came out of the palace and stood behind me, but I was too engrossed in my survival to bother looking at him.

"Mr. Sylvester." A deep voice, authoritative. "I am so terribly sorry for these events." The accent was all Prince Charles robed in African hues. British universities had done wonders for him. Saluso. State governor, client, disaffected ex-presidential candidate.

"Why be sorry, Governor? It was all for my protection,

wasn't it?" I said, looking at the ground, too tired to bother lifting my head. He wasn't worth a look in the eye anyway.

"Admittedly you have every right for anger," he said. "What we have done with you is too far from standard proceedings." I raised my eyes, squinting, as he descended the steps and came around to stand in front of me. He had a strong face, rectangular with solid bones that contrasted sharply with his body, which was abnormally thin. To my eyes he measured about five foot four. Even in that heat, he wore a jacket and tie.

"I've already decided to triple our fee," I said.

He sat down on the step next to me and said, "Your sense of humor is most commendable considering the distresses you have endured."

"Get me something to drink," I said. As if by ESP, a servant appeared with cold lemonade for the two of us. The first glass went down fast, the second slower.

"Is it better?" Saluso still had the look of concern on his face, as if it bothered him that he'd done such a battering job on the merchandise he was buying with cold cash. "If you can manage it, we could go inside where I have installed air conditionings."

"Just like the car?"

"I concede the error." He smiled. "We will need to arrange for several repairs before we try such a hiding place again."

The man was smooth and slippery—pure butter. From the looks of the exterior of his palace, he had unlimited wealth. Did he have power to match?

I followed him inside. The interior was a perfect comple-
ment to the exterior—opulent to the point of being ridiculously showy. Carpet everywhere. Hardwood walls. Expensive
paintings. Chandeliers. Mozart gliding through an invisible
sound system.

He was watching for my reaction, and I guess I looked
suitably impressed without fawning. The room he showed me
to could have housed a tennis court with room for spectators.

You need to understand that I wasn't taken in by him.
Saluso was a snake, a nasty little gangster dressed up fit to kill
and sporting the best British education ill-gotten money
could buy. I had no doubts about the character of the man,
and his wealth only confirmed my convictions.

What he wanted from me was equally obvious. I didn't
buy the story that sneaking me out of the airport in the trunk
of a limo was for my protection. By using a bribed federal
official, he'd caused me to vanish. No one but his own people
would know where I was, which meant they could use me for
whatever dirty purpose they wanted.

There could be only one goal worthy of someone like
Saluso, and since another federal election wasn't due for three-
and-a-half years, he was unlikely to be polite about fulfilling
his dream. Somewhere in the mix was a plan for a coup, and
he wanted me to play some role in it.

All this, of course, put my consulting job in a whole different ballpark from the one Saluso claimed to be playing in.
Forget that I probably wouldn't be seeing my family by
Saturday. This was the kind of job my company was constantly
trying to avoid—megalomaniacs who had no idea how to

operate by the rules. I'd told Simpson that a mission like this could only turn into disaster, but he'd sent me anyway. Seeing Saluso's palace convinced me that my concerns were dead on.

The key was to play dumb. I'd been doing it for years all around the world, and I'd saved myself thousands in unpaid bribes. Sure, I could jump on Saluso's plot and tell him there was no way I was going to help him engineer a coup. But I needed elbow room to think about the kind of leverage he planned to use against me. It wasn't likely that he'd try to rush me into his game, so I had time to work on my strategy. Probably there'd be an attempted honeymoon so he could show me what a terrific guy he was, hoping he could convert me to his cause.

For my part, I had to get out of the palace, link up with Karen and the kids, and flee the country. The way Saluso had arranged to have me snatched made it clear that he was ready to use most any means to get me to do his bidding. I'd be a fool not to try to bail out.

Getting away was such a simple proposition that it hardly needed thinking about. Why should I worry that white faces were few and far between or that Saluso had probably bought and paid for every living person in his state? So what if my mere appearance on the street would have every black Mtobean staring and pointing? I had the Ben Sylvester optimism working for me.

And God. Don't forget God. As I lay in bed late that night (after a shower, then incredible French cuisine and small-talk about the glories of America), I took inventory of my resources, starting with the spiritual ones.

First, I was convinced that Karen's faith was true. I'd thrown myself on the mercy of her Master and put myself under his control. Second, I was changing inside so profoundly that I hardly believed it all. Third, I was a baby disciple riding on his wife's coattails for the most part and far from ready to fly on my own through a storm. Now Karen was miles away.

I spent a lot of time that first night praying. It was awkward and forced me into the still unfamiliar role of needing someone vastly greater than me. But I had no other resources.

My gut feeling was that Saluso was up to no good. He also had a great deal of power. Simpson's brief had told me that the man came from some obscure village, distinguished himself at school, was sent to England for doctoral work, and came back a full-blown physicist.

But life in the lab had grown boring for him. In his spare time, he gathered a circle of influential friends and spent his evenings entertaining them with long monologues about the proper way to reform government and bring new hope to the people.

Eventually he'd been elected state governor. Within two years, he ran for president of the country. That's where his story got interesting. Saluso, or so it appeared, devised a scheme to rig the election in his favor. But someone blew the whistle, and Saluso's opponents wrecked his plans by arranging for a UN team to supervise the vote. Not unexpectedly, Saluso didn't have the goods to win on his own.

Of course, he proclaimed far and wide that he'd been robbed, even that the UN officials had been corrupt. But most westerners saw this as nothing more than the posturing of a poor loser. Most, except for Libertec, my employer.

From what I could see of the man and his tactics so far, democracy was the farthest thing from Saluso's mind. He wanted power—raw and unchecked. The fact that they'd sent me anyway showed that Libertec's administration needed some serious housecleaning. This wasn't the first time they'd left me hanging in a bad spot, and no paycheck was worth the risks I was taking.

The other factor was Sid Murphy. When I'd known him at college, he was moody, quiet, a guy who craved a lot of attention but was too proud to go begging for it. Sid was brilliant in his own way, but off-beat, never playing by the rules. Even the mediocre B.A. they grudgingly gave him didn't kill his dream of getting filthy rich and retiring young to a desert island.

Incredibly, he seemed to have made it for the most part— apparently sole owner of a luxury hotel on the beach. But strip away the surface paint and the illusion was obvious. From what I could see, Sid Murphy was Saluso's lackey, and Saluso had probably bankrolled the guy's dream hotel. My old pal Sid got everything he wanted and all he had to do was sell his soul to the governor. Too bad I'd ever met him.

After a lot of tossing, I finally slept. Whatever the actual content of my dreams, I seemed to spend the whole night chasing after impossibly difficult tasks, fear mounting every second.

Morning. Waking to Mozart and wondering if I could carry on with this without throttling the little creep Saluso. Hating myself for dragging my family into it.

Praying. I found myself, white-knuckled, grabbing onto a God I barely knew. I couldn't see any way to escape Mtobe, let alone get Karen and the kids out.

Breakfast was poached eggs on toast, smoked salmon on the side, silver service. Saluso actually came to my room to show me the way to the dining room. Since the morning was wet and cool, he'd dressed in high-fashion sweater and slacks, at least $400 worth.

"Mr. Sylvester," he said, beaming at me as he prepared to devour a forkful of toast, "I want you to understand my vision for this great land."

I smiled back at him, a piece of poached egg in the back of my throat taking a long time to go down.

Everything he said to me was exactly what I expected— the problems of his people were solely due to the multinational exploiters. Saluso had the answer, and he was willing to sacrifice a brilliant scientific career to give himself to the people. Honestly, the guy must have had more than that going for him, but I didn't hear it. Just the shallow, old-fashioned ravings of a man who apparently believed he was God in the making, ready to redeem the chosen people from their oppressors.

"And so, Mr. Sylvester," he concluded, "I would greatly desire to show you what we have done to this state under the fulfillment of my ideas. We can perform a sort of guided tour. Would you be interested?"

"There's no need to impress me, Governor," I said. "If you say you have good ideas, I believe you. What I need to understand is what you want from me."

"My driver is ordered to be here in twenty minutes, to give you opportunity to prepare for the day," he answered. The thought crossed my mind that they'd write on his tombstone, "I did it my way, and so did everyone else."

Back in my room, time short, I lay on the bed and tried to assess what was going on. I was Saluso's kidnap victim and Sid Murphy had Karen and the kids. They probably weren't hostages yet, but they might be if I didn't cooperate with whatever Saluso had up his sleeve.

How deep was Sid Murphy into Saluso's game? I could go on batting this around forever, but I just didn't know. I had to assume that Saluso's wishes would carry more weight with Murphy than any shallow friendship Sid and I may have had so many years ago.

I heard the car pull up, and I went out into the damp of another muggy day. The rainy season had begun and the morning was cool, but the relief wouldn't last. Saluso continued to look crisp, obviously refusing to allow the climate to affect him.

This time we got into a far smaller car, a Peugeot, the tinted glass, the air conditioning, and the driver (a new man I'd not seen before) the only concessions to Saluso's greatness. As we rode out of the palace grounds, Saluso reminded his driver that he was on probation, with only one more mistake standing between him and unemployment. It was all done in English for my benefit.

"Yes, sir," the driver said.

"I'm terribly sorry, Mr. Sylvester," Saluso said to me. "These domestic problems are too troubling, but the alternative is to be sitting at table with anarchy as your guest."

I said nothing, watching the scenery, my eyes probing for some sign that I could get out of there safely. What I saw wasn't heartening. The palace was on the edge of a well-populated city—call it Port Daniels, Saluso's capital. What was more, there were no white faces in the crowd. Traveling unnoticed would be out of the question unless I had a tinted-window car like this one.

"How far are we from the national capital?" I asked, watching the chaos that masqueraded as traffic, wondering how so many cars could navigate side by side through such narrow streets.

"About seventy miles by road," Saluso told me. "We, however, are following a different path. My wish is to take you to the place where I was born."

Great. This was going to be one of those "let me show you the monuments to my past out of which my greatness came" sessions. Something I'd said must have convinced Saluso he was dealing with an idiot.

Port Daniels was a wonder of contradictions, sporting everything from fabulous mansions to tar paper hovels, from large modern department stores to row after row of tiny market stalls. Nothing was planned, but the whole mix of life, noisy beyond belief, worked together as if it were a single complex organism, throbbing with vitality. There was a rhythm to it that could easily become addicting.

I saw women wearing the latest Paris fashions counterfeited from magazine pictures, old men riding in from the countryside on decrepit bicycles piled with produce, children in uniforms shuffling unwillingly off to school, middle-aged women carrying five gallon water containers on turbaned heads. From enormous loudspeakers in market stalls, I could hear the sound of an old Jim Reeves cowboy tune telling the world about the woman who done him wrong. Every intersection brought out an assortment of hawkers banging on car windows, hoping we'd buy whatever pitiful wares they carried around with them.

This was Saluso's turf, and I wondered whether any Westerner could ever really comprehend it. There's something about Africa that defies all attempts at explanation, a logic to the whole place that works beyond the normal bounds of rational analysis.

We left the city behind and headed northeast on a secondary paved road with potholes and crumbling edges. "Where I was born" was likely to be some crummy village in the bush after a two day hike through the mud. There were people along the road, on the road, working on farms carved out of the palm jungle. Every farm was a small patch of serious agriculture, intensively cultivated. Traffic was still horrendous, mainly taxis driven by men who had never heard of highway regulations.

After twenty miles of the same, with the driver leaning almost constantly on the horn, the farms began to thin out and the jungle thickened. A short while later, we turned off the paved road onto a narrow dirt track. At least, it had been a dirt track in the dry season. Now it was a stream, a minimum of six inches deep, with firm ground only occasionally emerging, red-brown, for a gulp of air. Saluso, who had said nothing for a long time, murmured, "This is my home."

There wasn't any home, just thick jungle with a sub-merged pathway cutting through it. In minutes we were sur-rounded by trees and vines, plowing through an ever-deepening flood. I could feel water rushing under the floorboards, and Saluso began whining at the driver, telling him what parts to avoid, where to slow down, where to speed up, finally where to get out and wade around the corner because there may have been a washout. The poor man came back soaked to the thighs.

"It is all no problem, no problem, Excellency," he said. "We run to the left." His voice gave no sign of the frustration he must have been feeling. The prestige of being the gover-nor's driver was worth a few indignities along the way.

I estimated we were at least eight miles into the jungle when the road suddenly opened. To my amazement, there was a clearing, about three-quarters of a mile across, ringed by mud and thatch houses. In the middle was a school and an enormous stone church in English cathedral style.

It was the church that caught my attention, or rather its stained-glass windows. I'm not joking. There they were—large depictions of the life of Christ, at least four per side, presum-ably sixteen in all.

"How did that get here?" I asked, angry at myself for let-ting Saluso impress me again.

"We have a long tradition of missionaries, Mr. Sylvester," Saluso said. "Just because we have taken our journey into the forest does not demand that we should be 'in the backwoods' as you Americans would describe it."

Score one for Saluso. Maybe we were more of a pair than I thought. Whatever Saluso's motives in bringing me, I had a feeling I was about to learn something.

CHAPTER FOUR

BEN

The people of the village were enthralled with Saluso. Within minutes the fatted lamb was slaughtered and turning on a spit, while the entire village, maybe a thousand strong, gathered around the steps of the church where Saluso had established an impromptu platform.

"My friends," he began. "My family. It is so good to be back in my home. For eight months I have thought of you with longing, but my many duties have kept me from you." After this he lapsed into his native language. From the crowd came laughter, shouts, rumbles of approval. Saluso the hero.

Half an hour later, he started to wind down, a short speech by African standards. It seemed to me he was doing nothing more than fulfilling social requirements, as if he had something more important on his mind. As I watched him from the edge of the crowd, his posturing and the way he basked in the adulation of the villagers enhanced my contempt for this little man. For the life of me, I couldn't understand why my bosses, especially Simpson, chief of operations, had taken this one on. Saluso seemed to me to be a potential time bomb.

As he came down the steps of the church, I noticed a change come over him for an instant, a shedding of his public face to reveal a tired, more somber one underneath. As soon as he reached ground level, he called over his driver and gave him some instruction. The driver hurried off through the crowd while Saluso, his public face firmly back on, shook hands with well-wishers, pausing in the midst of each handshake as if to emphasize how dear the person was to him.

I waited, taking it in, watching the crowd bunching up to shake his hand, still wondering what had brought me here. Why didn't the man just get on with it and tell me, "Mr. Sylvester, I want you to help me plan a coup and establish my very own dictatorship. Then, perhaps, you can rejoin your family" (with stress on "perhaps").

The driver came back in a rush, and after a brief conversation with Saluso, took his arm and led him along a beaten track that went behind the church. I followed and so did everyone else. At the edge of the clearing, a path led a couple of hundred yards to a fairly large house of cement blocks.

"Mr. Sylvester, I want you to meet him," Saluso said, beaming at me. "I hoped he would be at the church, but they say he is feeling the pain in his bones and stayed at home today."

"Who?"

"Reverend Craven." Saluso clapped his hands twice sharply, and after a few seconds, a small, shriveled man shuffled out of the cement house. I was amazed. Craven, living there in the deepest part of the jungle, was a white man.

"Who is this?" The voice that came out of him was soft, mellow, like a BBC announcer, and when he looked me in the eye, I could sense his intelligence and integrity.

"Ben Sylvester." I stuck out my hand. "Did you build that church over there?" I asked.

"Not entirely by myself. Do you like it?"

"Very much," I told him, disarmed by his obvious decency.

"I'm Donald Craven. I suppose you're surprised to find a white man this deep in the jungle. Most people are."

There was an awkward pause while we sized each other up.

"Reverend Craven has given his entire life to my people," Saluso said. "What is more, this man is my father."

Craven smiled. "Not in the biological sense, Mr. Sylvester."

"Ben," I said.

"Ben. When he was young, Songo worked for me after his parents died of fever."

Songo. Songo Saluso. The name had a certain melody to it.

"Reverend Craven raised me, and I owe everything to him, even my schooling, my desire to serve this nation. Everything." To my surprise, Saluso seemed close to tears.

"He came with a lot of natural talent, believe me," Craven said, waving a hand in dismissal. "I was happy just to have an—"

He stopped as a small commotion went through the crowd and someone came running with a message for Saluso. "Radio phone call," Saluso explained to me, looking every bit the man of importance. "There are no vacations for servants of the people."

As soon as Saluso left, I grabbed Craven's shirt sleeve and whispered in his ear, "We have to talk."

Without hesitation, Craven turned to the people crowded on the trail and shouted, "We are going inside to wait. Governor Saluso will no doubt speak to you later."

His house was simple, even drab, little furniture, a few landscape reproductions (all of them of England) on the walls. There appeared to be three or four large rooms plus an outbuilding in the back serving as his kitchen. Not much to show for all his years of service.

He offered me a tattered armchair in his living room, taking the other one made of bamboo. The room was big enough for a party of ten, but the only other furniture in it was a small end table.

I found myself looking into a shrewd face. Craven was gracious enough, but he wasn't going to let very much get by him.

"You're eager to tell me that Governor Saluso is a megalomaniac who's plotting a coup," he said.

"You know?"

"Sometimes, Mr. Sylvester—"

"Ben."

"Sometimes, Ben, we believe what's easiest to believe. Songo's messenger told me a few minutes ago that you've come here to help him win the next election. If that's the case, you really need to listen to him rather than to the rumor-mongers."

"All I've heard from Saluso are platitudes."

"I won't deny that he's arrogant, with a desire for power. But he means what he's saying. He loves this country and its people."

"Reverend Craven, what's the point of defending him? I realize you have a personal interest in Saluso, but there's very little question about the nature of his plans."

"They're obvious to you?"

"Of course."

Craven smiled, but there was no humor in his eyes. "If he's so dangerous, why do you think the federal government hasn't arrested him?"

"They're still gathering evidence."

"Don't be naive, Ben. Listen to Songo."

"If you've got any information that will help me, please let me have it. Look, if it makes any difference, I'm a follower of Christ just like you." I felt uneasy playing on our common faith.

"Let me tell you about Songo." Craven stretched one leg out and started flexing his knee. "Arthritis," he explained. "I must keep mobile." I sensed that he was in a fair amount of pain. "Long before Songo became governor, he started working to bring health care to the smaller villages. You may not be aware of this, but most trained nurses and doctors would much rather practice in the cities where they have good facilities and better salaries. The public health service constantly goes begging for personnel."

"It happens everywhere," I said.

"When Songo was in England working on his doctorate, he found two medical students from Mtobe and convinced them to work with him to establish rotating clinics all over the state. When he became governor, he purged much of the corruption out of the civil service and diverted the savings into water projects and improved agriculture, raising the people out of the malnutrition they'd suffered for centuries. When the government funding wasn't enough, he gave up most of his own salary and at least half of the money normally used to staff the governor's mansion. It all went into help for the people."

"Then why does he come off like some banana republic potentate?"

"Appearances only. In Africa you're looked down upon if you have wealth or power and you refuse to flaunt it. Songo has strong ambitions, but the only power he wants is the power to help his people."

"Then how did he manage to lose the federal election?"

"It was his bad choice of friends."

"What friends?"

He paused and looked at me appraisingly. "The next time you're alone with him, Ben, ask him who controls the Young Pioneers program in this state."

"The Young Pioneers? Didn't that used to be the Commie version of the Boy Scouts with military training thrown in?"

"Ask him. Press him on it. In fact, ask him why a decent man who loves his people would become entangled with evil power seekers."

"Why don't you tell me yourself?"

He hesitated before he spoke. "I came to this place fifty years ago, and except for furloughs and insurrections, I've never left it. The government has given me a permanent residency permit. Goodness knows, at my age I had few friends in England to go back to. One brother, but he has the means to visit me here whenever he wants to."

"You never married?"

"Oh yes. Yellow fever took her six months after we first came to the village."

"I'm sorry."

"It was long ago. What I'm trying to tell you is that this village and its people are very precious to me."

"Would you or this village be at risk if you were to tell me what's really going on with Saluso?"

"I've already told you that Songo isn't planning a coup. But there is a threat here nevertheless."

"What threat?" My frustration probably showed.

"Ask who runs the Young Pioneers. Ask him why they have a training base only three miles from here. Ask him why a white man is the richest person in the state. I—" Craven broke off as Saluso walked in, his presence immediately occupying the remaining free space in the room.

"Dreadfully sorry, Ben," Saluso said. "Some matters are not to be avoided."

"It's all right."

Craven looked worried, intense. What kind of chemistry was working between him and Saluso? I couldn't see how Songo could be anything other than the snake I took him for, despite all the social programs Craven had told me about. There was too much pride in the man, too much drive for personal power.

"You must see the church," Saluso said, his tone like that of a child about to show off some great treasure to his best friend. "Reverend Craven designed it and directed in the constructing. It is a work of art."

It was. As Saluso and I walked across the compound, the big stone structure dominated our vision. Inside, the dark hardwood pews, built to seat at least eight hundred, warmed the severity of the stone walls. At the front, there was a wrap-around hardwood pulpit, ornately carved with scenes from the Gospels. Then there were the stained glass windows that refracted colored light onto the stone floors.

Saluso took on a quiet mood. He walked up into the pulpit and stood there, tiny, overpowered by the size of the thing. I waited below, halfway up the center aisle.

"I grew to be a man in this church, Ben," he began, his voice sounding tired. "When my parents died and Reverend Craven claimed me as a son, every thought of ours rested on this church and the people who came to do their worship here. There was work to do, too much work, and school here in the village. We were living within the Reverend Craven's passion to teach the love of Jesus to these people."

He stared at me until I grew uneasy, then went on with his sermon.

"I was nurtured with a fire in my heart to serve, to be doing something to soothe the pain of those around me. I know, Ben"—he waved his hand—"you think of me as a charlatan with a lion's hunger for power." I kept my mouth shut. "My beginnings were in physics. I suppose I hoped to develop the sort of technology that would raise our nation to health and much prosperity." Great. A life story. Saluso must have been a whiz at parties. "But I turned to politics when I saw that all of our movings forward were only making heavy the pockets of the elite. There had to be a better path."

"Marxism?"

"I am sorry?" he said, not catching my drift.

"Marxism might have spread the wealth."

"Marxism can never succeed in Africa. Africans are too attracted by the power of the common man to sell his own goods and reap many profits for himself. They would resist forced organizations and collectives."

"What was your better way?"

"At the beginning I had very few ideas, but I gathered a circle of wise friends around me. We saw that rising to the task of governor might be profitable, but that I would only be truly able to help my people if I became president of Mtobe. I know that you will believe my only motivation is the craving for power, but power for me is only a path to—"

"That's why you tried to rig the election? To guarantee you'd have the power to do good?"

"No. That was not my work at all."

"The UN observers did it?"

"I fear, Ben, that though you are professional in political advisings, your reasoning scarcely will rise above that of a small boy." Saluso leaned forward over the enormous pulpit, his body ridiculously dwarfed by it. "I suppose I am to be served up as the villain who will do anything to ascend to the throne. Are you taking me for a fool as well?"

"Governor Saluso," I said, anger rising, "I didn't ask for this trip. I told my employers that they should turn you down flat. In fact, I don't remember asking for anything from you except to be told what you want me to do. If you don't want to tell me what your secret is, then you can hardly blame me for believing what people are saying about you."

"Your point is well taken, Ben." Saluso sighed audibly and climbed down from his perch. He sat down on the front pew, and I sat opposite him on the steps leading up to the pulpit. After a moment, he hunched forward and put his forehead in his hands, elbows on his knees. Suddenly he was tiny and vulnerable.

"When I became governor," he said, "we were a number of friends, little more. Somehow we had captured the imagination of our people and they voted for us. Suddenly we were too overwhelmed in every manner. We possessed too few representatives with any proper experience, and too little money."

"You asked yourself what you could have been thinking of running for office when all you really knew anything about was physics."

"How could you know that?"

"It's my field," I said. "I've walked lots of politicians through their self-doubt. But you don't seem to have the same problem now."

"I did, Ben. I scarcely had an idea where to turn. I came back here to my village, to talk with Reverend Craven, but he could only pray for me. Too much more was needed."

"You could have called my company. We specialize in helping new governments function."

"I had no money to pay such consultants."

"Yet now, four or five years later, in your second term as governor, you're rolling in wealth."

"Appearances only. My home is the official house of the

governor. The cars and servants are paid for by the many taxes of the people."

"How did you go on to bankroll a presidential campaign?"

Saluso turned his head away and got up. He walked slowly to the nearest window, a stained glass of Christ blessing the children. For over a minute he stared at it.

"This is too embarrassing." He turned to me. "No, it is far more terrible, a personal humiliation. This very moment has been filling me with dread for many days, but I know that it is necessary to tell you truly of my history."

I waited, but Saluso had gone silent. "Governor?" He said nothing. "Who runs your youth program for you?"

"How have you heard of my youth program?"

"Reverend Craven told me to ask you."

What little power Saluso had worn seemed to fall off him as if it were an old coat, big and heavy, with the pockets full. He stood exposed.

"When I won the governorship," he began, sitting back down on the pew, "I found a small moment to be alone, and I wept. It was not joy in my heart, you understand. It was fear. None of us truly did believe that we would win."

"You found someone to help you. A benefactor."

He looked surprised for a second. "A man came to my house. He had much money and the ownership of many people."

"People?"

"A network, let us say, of important men of loyalty who would not falter in a storm."

"Bribed people."

"You make it sound too sordid."

"Not at all. Who were they—judges, army officers, police?"

"I did not ask him. He only told me that he could bless me with the support of many great men in my state, men of weight and importance."

"He bribed them all?"

"Of course not. They are his friends. Favors were being earned, and perhaps favors were being returned."

"How long did it take your benefactor to gain control over you?" I asked.

"He promised me that I would not have to cast aside any of my dreams."

"Were you that naive?"

"Yes!" Sudden anger. "Yes, I believed that man, and then he became my master."

"How? What leverage did he have?"

"I needed the funds he was offering and the great men who could help me."

"For that you sold out to him?"

"If you wish to call it that."

"He funded your run for federal office?"

"Yes."

"Was fixing the election his idea?" I felt like an interrogator. He made it easy with his hangdog humility.

"Yes."

"He had that much power over you?"

"One night soon after we met, I was telling him about this village and of its exceeding value to me. He...you must please understand that every man may be purchased or sold if the right price is agreed upon. The price for me was not money."

"He threatened to harm this village?"

"You have seen how deep we are within the jungle. People can disappear from this place."

"What did he tell you?"

"Nothing clearly. He told me only about the great importance of a man's home. He offered to pay much money for extra troops to protect us from harm. Then he brought young men to an encampment near here to make them Young Pioneers, and the people of this village could hear their guns as he trained them in military skills."

"Are you sure it was a threat?"

"You cannot have a knowledge of this man or you would not ask such a question." He paused, then smiled. "Ah, but you do know this man."

"I do?"

"Ponder it. The answer must now be obvious to you."

"Look, I've been patient enough for Job. Stop playing games with me."

"His name is Sid Murphy."

CHAPTER FIVE

K A R E N

From a distance Karen could hear Jimmie screaming with a high-pitched wail a mother instantly recognizes as her child in pain. She jumped out of her chair before Sid Murphy could even start to get up, then turned to give Sid a reproachful look. "I thought someone was looking after my kids."

She reached Jimmie quickly, but it turned out to be only a shell cut on the bottom of his foot. Just a scratch. It couldn't be helped, she thought. But maybe, Lord, you could have a little mercy on an innocent child. She picked Jimmie up and carried him, crying, back to the hotel. With a small first aid kit she got from the desk clerk, she bandaged him.

Jimmie always rebounded quickly. It wasn't more than ten minutes before he was off playing with Jack again. The man who was supposed to be watching them followed them discreetly. Karen went back to the patio where she'd been trying to reason with Sid Murphy.

"You told me Ben would be here today," she said. "Where is he?"

"With the governor," Murphy said. "What's the big deal about this, Karen? You knew he had a job to do. I told you it would be done Saturday, but I guess it's taking longer."

"Then let me phone him."

"Oh sure, I'm going to spend four hours going through all Saluso's aides only to find out he's too busy to talk. It's not like we're such great buddies that I can call him up anytime I want."

"Couldn't you try anyway?"

"Give it a couple more days. There's nothing to worry about."

Karen went back down to the beach to watch her kids. She found it strange to have this perfect hotel on a perfect world-class beach at the edge of a nation scarcely born. Even a telephone call was a big deal.

Not that she wanted to criticize them. The people of Mtobe had suffered under colonialism and survived it. Why should they be expected to operate by western standards now?

Karen checked on Jimmie again. He was having so much fun he'd already forgotten the cut on his foot. She prayed again for Ben, even while her mind kept refusing to admit that they were in the midst of yet another terrible time. Weak as she felt, she asked God to spare them from harm.

There weren't any other westerners in the hotel. In fact, there were few guests at all—some Arabs and a few rich Africans with their girlfriends.

For the past four days, Karen and the kids had been left pretty much on their own. Sid was always busy with one thing or another. They'd taken comfortable rounds of beach and pool and playroom, even videos for the kids. The meals were strange. Apparently the African cook was trying to cook western style and had little respect for its nuances. Karen would have been happier eating African food.

The only friendly face they saw was the bellhop, a man of about thirty who showed the kind of intelligence that led Karen to believe he'd taken the job only until he could find something that matched his gifts.

The fellow's name was Kdoma, whether his first name or last Karen had no idea. He seemed to want to befriend them from the day they arrived. At first Karen thought it was she. She may have had a few years behind her, but she knew she could still turn heads.

Kdoma showed them where everything was, explained the meal procedures, and led the kids on exploring trips around the hotel. Sid, though, didn't like the extra attention Kdoma was giving them. After three days, he told Kdoma to stay inside the hotel, then he assigned his own man to watch the kids whenever the family was outside.

It was near midnight on Saturday, while they were asleep, the boys in the double bed near Karen's, that someone came into their room. They were on the fifth floor, and she'd left a window open to give them some of the cooler night air. She must have been very tired because the first thing she knew, a rough hand had been clamped over her mouth.

She panicked, struggling, but he was too strong for her. For a few seconds, she couldn't breathe at all, and then he eased up a bit on the pressure of his hand. "Please," a voice hissed in her ear, "I want to help you." When she took hold of his hand to pull it from her mouth, he hung on, even though her nails dug into his skin. "It's Kdoma," he said. "Please."

Surprised, she stopped struggling, and gradually his palm lifted off her mouth. She could still barely see him, only his shadow.

"What are you doing here?" she whispered between gasps.

"I must remove you. You and your boys. Tonight."

"You've been watching too much American television," she said, angry for the way he'd frightened her.

"Mr. Murphy is too dangerous. I must now bring you to your husband."

"What are your saying?"

"Please," he said. "I am in the employment of the governor."

"You work for Governor Saluso? Why are you here then? What do you know about my husband?"

"The governor sent me to watch over you. I made Mr. Murphy to believe that I was a police officer under the direction of the federal government, and thus he felt compelled to employ me. To turn me away would invite suspicion."

"No, what I meant was, why are you here in my room in the middle of the night?"

"I have already told you—we must flee. There are many many reasons for believing you are not safe any longer."

"What if I want to stay here?" she asked. "How do I know you really want to help us? What if I report you to Mr. Murphy?" Kdoma had scared her. What proof did she have that he wasn't going to take them out and hurt them?

"You refuse to come?"

"Yes, I do. I can't move from this hotel until I have some clear word from my husband."

Karen asked him to leave and he went, looking discouraged. Clearly she couldn't trust Sid Murphy, but could she trust Kdoma just because he'd been nice to them? Even prayer gave her little comfort.

In the morning, after a long night of thinking and worrying and trying to talk to a confusing God, she got the kids up, and they went down to breakfast. On the way they met Kdoma, and he got into the elevator with them, scarcely acknowledging them except to whisper to Karen as he got off at the next floor. "I'll bring evidence."

She looked at him, and he returned her stare calmly, then turned and walked down the hallway. She kept on staring after Kdoma until the elevator doors closed again, and they went the rest of the way to the main floor dining room.

Sid Murphy was waiting with a big smile on his face. As usual, he hadn't shaved for a couple of days. "I've reached him, Mrs. Sylvester," he told Karen. "Ben will be here tomorrow. Apparently the governor is pleased with his help."

"Good," she said. "I've been very worried."

"Pretty calm reaction for someone who loves her husband dearly. You and Ben having problems?" She had a fleeting urge to slap him, but she didn't even frown for fear of revealing that she didn't believe a word he was telling her.

As soon as they'd finished breakfast, Karen took the kids to the beach. They never seemed to tire of the sand and seashells and water that was like a comfortable bath. True, it was the wet season, and they usually had to run for shelter at least once a day. The clouds, when they rolled in, took the edge off the heat, but in this tropical climate it never got too cool for people from Washington State.

Sid Murphy's servant, a hard man who'd never told them his name, shadowed them. Karen couldn't remember him having said anything to them, and he always wore a jacket or sweater, no matter how warm it was. All the better to conceal a weapon? Everything about him told Karen that he'd spent time in the military.

That morning he seemed more watchful, scanning the sea and staring up the beach in both directions. But there was no one to look at except Karen and the kids. The beach was deserted and the sea was empty.

Jack and Jimmie ran right to the water and started romping in the waves. Karen thought of sharks and moved closer to them until the water was washing around her ankles. Murphy's servant stepped inside the ten foot circle he had mentally placed around them and stood beside her. His heavy boots were getting wet.

"Nice boys," he said. His words startled her.

"Excuse me?" she asked. "Oh yes, they're very precious to my husband and me."

"I have wanted to speak with you, Mrs. Sylvester." He spoke English well, but his African accent was thick. "Mr. Murphy and I are much concerned about this Kdoma, the servant who is to see to your needs. Has he said or done any things to offend?"

Jack and Jimmie had walked further down the beach, chasing each other and throwing small lumps of oil from an old spill. She watched them while she wondered what to say to Murphy's servant.

"Kdoma has been very helpful," she said, feeling guilty for saying nothing about his late night visit to their room. "Why? Has there been a problem?"

"We suspect he is a federal agent. That is not strange in this country, and we must accept him into our employment even though he spies on us."

"Why? Why must you accept him?"

"To refuse such a man would bring too much trouble to us all. The authorities would then send many more spies to us. But we worry now that this man is making difficulty for our guests."

The boys were quite far away, almost at the edge of the hotel property. Beyond them was only jungle and sand.

"I'm not sure I understand why a federal agent would be spying on this hotel," she said, looking down the beach. "Don't you think we should bring the children back? They're wandering a bit far for my liking."

He turned quickly, uttered a string of words in his own language, and started running down the beach, shouting at the boys to come back. Her heart suddenly racing, Karen ran after him, her sandals flapping in the sand at every step.

Ahead of them the beach narrowed, with about fifty feet of sand between the water and the dense jungle. The children had gone past the narrow part and were staring up toward the jungle. What were they looking at? Wild animals? Snakes?

Murphy's servant ran desperately until he reached the boys, then he grabbed each of them roughly by an arm and started dragging them toward Karen.

"Stop that!" she shouted. He ignored her, so she ran faster. "Let go of my children!" she said, startling him so much he let go and turned back toward the hotel.

When she looked to see what had caught the kids' attention, she saw a building up in the jungle that looked like a barracks. She was about to ask Murphy's man what it was when some twenty soldiers burst out of the building, heavy weapons in their hands, and charged straight toward Karen and the boys.

She screamed and flung the kids to the sand, sheltering them with her body. Around them, she could hear feet tramping and rifle bolts clicking back.

"Don't shoot," she said. "Please." Please, no more.

Then there was only silence. She couldn't force herself to open her eyes or even raise her head.

"Mom, you're squishing me," Jimmie said, his voice muffled. She tried to lift some of her weight off him, but the second he felt some freedom he squirmed loose and stood up. "Who are you guys?" she heard him say.

"Get to your feet," a harsh voice said. They did what they were told. Soldiers encircled them, their guns pointed. Murphy's servant was standing in front of their leader. For awhile the two of them exchanged nasty words, the little captain showing that he was in charge while Sid Murphy's servant, who towered over him, did all he could to apologize. Then, abruptly, the soldiers pulled up their weapons and walked back to their barracks.

"Come with me," Sid Murphy's servant said to Karen

angrily. He marched her and the boys to the edge of the hotel property and pointed a shaking finger at a small sign with fading letters stuck into the sand. It read: "No guests beyond this point. Military area. Danger." Karen had been too busy chasing the kids even to notice it.

"You have made this very bad for me, Mrs. Sylvester," he said. "Very bad. I will not forget." His tone frightened her, and she felt herself shrinking from him.

"We're going back to the hotel now," she said. "Is that all right?"

He didn't answer, and so she took the kids' hands and they walked silently back to the hotel and then up to their room. Jimmie understood very little of what had happened, but Karen was afraid Jack would probably have nightmares.

They turned on the TV—another one of those endless panel discussions that are the staple of African television. It was time for all of them to go home. In the space of less than a week, they'd been shot at, set upon by a man in the dark, and almost killed by a squad of soldiers.

The kids found a few books Karen had brought with them and tried to occupy themselves. Five minutes later they were getting on each others' nerves again.

"Cut it out," Karen said, her voice too loud.

"When's Dad coming?" Jimmie asked for the hundredth time.

"Soon. Any day now," she answered.

When a knock came at the door, it was almost a relief. "Who's there?" Karen asked.

"Sid."

She opened the door.

"Hey kids," he said, "the cook's just prepared hamburgers U.S. style. Why don't you go down? Your mom will join you in a few minutes." They left eagerly.

Once Karen was alone with Sid Murphy, he wasted no time explaining why he'd come. "I'm afraid we're going to have to move you."

"Where? Why?" Her heart started to race, and she had to force herself to take a deep breath.

"Look, Mrs. Sylvester, I'm sorry I haven't been totally straight with you."

"You haven't? I'm shocked."

"We don't have to like each other, you know," he said. "Look, here's the deal. Those troops you saw today? They work for Governor Saluso. So does your bellhop, Kdoma. We're being squeezed, and I'm worried about your safety."

"But your servant told me he suspected that Kdoma works for the federal government."

"That's his opinion. He's wrong."

"And those people who shot at our car while we were on our way here from the airport?"

"I don't know. Honestly. I've got a few enemies. It could have been a random robbery attempt."

"Why does the governor keep troops next to your hotel?" she asked, her heart still beating very quickly.

"It's not my hotel."

"Why did twenty men point their guns at a woman and two little kids?" She could feel her fear rising.

"You weren't supposed to be there."

"Mr. Murphy, I'm so very tired of these games."

"Okay. In a nutshell—Saluso is a dangerous man who's putting plans together to take over the country. Maybe something worse."

"And what about you? In what way are you involved with Governor Saluso?"

"The hotel," he said.

"He owns this hotel?"

"No, it's owned by several oil companies. It's kind of embarrassing to admit this, but I was doing some industrial espionage in Kuwait a few years ago while I managed a small hotel as a front. When an oil company executive caught me filming documents, somebody thought I might be just the man for this job."

"I'm afraid I don't understand you."

"They set me up in this hotel to give me enough prominence in the state to get in thick with Saluso. I've been working on it since before he became governor. You see, oil is very big in this country, and the oil companies have seen Saluso as their biggest risk for a coup. They don't like coups, especially when there's a danger that the new government will nationalize the major industries."

"Can you tell me why my husband is here in this country?" she asked. "What does Governor Saluso want with him?"

"He brought Ben in to help plan a coup."

"What do you mean? Ben would never consent to something like that."

"He would if persuaded."

"You tricked Ben into coming here," she said. "How could you pretend to be his friend and then lure him here on the pretense that he was going to help with a democratic election? How could you let Governor Saluso steal Ben from us and not even do a thing to stop it?"

"It wasn't my idea," Murphy said. "At least I got the governor to agree to let you and the children stay here rather than at his mansion."

"And why did you help him at all when you knew what he wanted Ben for?"

"There wasn't any choice. Those soldiers from that barracks over there are on Saluso's payroll, and they aren't here on vacation. I don't relish storm troopers beating down my door in the wee hours of the night and then attaching electrodes to sensitive areas of my body. Look, I've got lots of resources. The oil companies have unlimited money, and the U.S. government is monitoring Saluso. We'll find a way to stop him."

"Where are you hoping to move us?" she asked.

"To a more secure place where Saluso can't get at us. I'll make sure Kdoma doesn't follow us either. Look, Karen, the only persuasion Saluso has over Ben is a threat to harm you and your kids. If he can't find you, he loses his edge. So are you going to cooperate or not?"

"Yes," she said.

CHAPTER SIX

BEN

There is some problem." Saluso thrust himself into the sitting room of his home, where I was reading a Raymond Chandler the day after our grand tour of the governor's accomplishments. The look on Saluso's face didn't assure me.

"Did the cook quit?" He wasn't used to whatever it was that passed for my sense of humor.

"Your wife…" he said, trailing off.

"What's happened to her?"

"I don't know." He sagged into a chair and put his head in his hands. "When Mr. Murphy first told me of his decision bringing you here, he required that your family would come with you. I had no opportunity to refuse—this man has all the power over me—but I pleaded with him to let your family lodge here where he did not have the means to treat them badly."

"Obviously your gifts of persuasion need some work. What power does he have?"

"The people he has bribed, the evidence that falsely connects me with evil schemes in the past election, his threat to my village. When he refused to let your family remain here, I sent a man from my own staff to look to their interests. I was too afraid of what Mr. Murphy might be doing. My man pretended that he was agent for the president, and Mr. Murphy feared not to accept him into his employment."

"Where is my family now?"

"I have no ideas. Gone."

"What about the person you sent to protect them? Was he napping? Drunk? What?"

"He is not superhuman. When he found that they are gone, he reported to me promptly and I have come immediately to you."

"So Murphy moved my family."

"Yes."

"Why?"

"I think he has discovered a proper understanding of your purpose in this place."

"Which is?" I got up and stood in front of him. He didn't look up. I waited. "What's your problem?" I asked, my voice louder than I'd expected. "You tell me you're on the up and up, that you're some kind of prisoner of the evil Murphy. But every time I ask you why I'm here, you launch into some eulogy about your country or you take me on a field trip like that little jaunt to the village yesterday. If you want me to help you, you've got to level with me. What do you want from me?"

"You are here, Mr. Sylvester..." He looked up, his eyes shining. "You are here to free me of this man forever."

"You want me to get rid of Sid? Forgive me, Governor,

but I'm having a hard time figuring out your devious little scheme. Let me get this straight. Sid was the man who insisted on you hiring me, but he doesn't know you've turned against him."

"Correct, but I fear he suspects now."

"So what did Murphy think I was coming here to do?"

"I revealed to him a certain hunger for the presidency," Saluso said. "He believes that we engaged you to help us plan an armed coup. Or, more correctly, he was believing that."

"Now for some reason he's starting to suspect that you've turned against him?"

"Yes. Something has happened. I cannot know what it is."

"Has he moved my family so he can make them hostages?"

"I am certain they are safe. In moving your family, he was preparing a slight warning for me, that is all. He is telling me to be careful not to betray him. I cannot find reason for Mr. Murphy being suspicious of me. I was doing what he told me—to convince you to help prepare a plan for me."

"For the coup."

"Yes."

"What did you think I could contribute? Surely you and Murphy have enough cunning between you to set up a coup."

"Mr. Murphy does not want it to fail. He insisted that we needed someone with political knowledge to help us foresee any errors."

"And why would I have done that for you? I work for a reputable company. We're not into armed insurrections."

"Mr. Murphy told me that you could be available for our

use if we offered you sufficient money. I was to give you fifty thousand U.S. dollars."

"So why haven't you?"

"Because I have no desire for a coup. That was all Mr. Murphy's desire."

"You must have known that my family would be bargaining chips. It's a cinch Murphy didn't invite them here because he was feeling generous. What in the world were you thinking, dragging a woman and children into a mess like this?"

"When we arranged for you to come to us, Mr. Murphy ordered that your family must visit us as well. I was not able to persuade him against this."

"You were willing to barter away the lives of a woman and two little kids…" There didn't seem to be anything more to say to the man. But I needed more answers than I was getting if I was ever to make sense of things. "Why have you told me this instead of letting me go on believing that my family was safe at the hotel? Do you honestly think I'm going to help you now that I know Murphy controls the people I love?"

Saluso's face slipped into neutral, as if I'd turned off whatever it was that animated him, his eyes suddenly dark and cold. "I am expending considerable efforts to have you here, Mr. Sylvester," he said. "If you refuse to help me remove the influence of Mr. Murphy, I will have you disappear. The records will show that you left along with your wife and sons. Only you and I and a small group of my friends will know your fate. As to your wife and children, they can be left in the hands of Mr. Murphy."

Finally the gloves were off. "So you're no more than a two-bit gangster after all," I said softly.

He looked sad, not angry. "The furthest thing from my real desire is to bring harm to you and your family," he said. "I had hoped that after you visited my village and saw the work I am doing for my people—"

"That I would be overwhelmed with fervor for your country and its future? Be serious, Mr. Saluso. As far as I'm concerned, you should have stayed in your lab where you might have done some good. As a politician, you're nothing short of incompetent."

That struck a nerve. I thought he was going to launch himself at my throat, but his British-trained manners won the day. He only smiled, a wide grimace in his tiny face.

"Insults will not solve our problems, Ben. My only motivation in seeking your help is to free myself of this white man so that he will not force me to partake in his coup. Mr. Murphy, as you are no doubt aware, is defective in personality, and his hunger to rule Mtobe is very dangerous."

"Are you saying that Murphy is the one who wants the power? That he intends for you to be some kind of front for him?"

"We are an African country, Ben. Mr. Murphy has known that we would never accept a white man as president. He desires the power, not the recognition. I unfortunately have become his puppet."

"Who's funding him?"

"Mr. Murphy tells me it is the oil companies. Our president has taxed them too severely, and they fear losing all of their profits. Mr. Murphy has convinced them that I am the superior of the candidates for ruler of Mtobe."

"Do they know their money is paying for a coup?"

"No doubt they suspect this. But the taxes are making too much suffering for them. Mr. Murphy has told them they will pay only half taxes if I am ruler."

"Will they?"

"Mr. Murphy is too devious. He will compel me to nationalize all the oil workings in the country."

"Turn on the very people who funded you?"

"Yes, I fear."

"All of that aside for the moment," I said, struggling with my anger, "let me understand this—you are determined that I'm going to help you free yourself of Murphy. If I refuse, my family disappears without a trace and I probably end up with a bullet in the head."

"You express yourself too distastefully, Ben."

"If I help you," I went on, "Murphy will find out eventually that I'm working against him. Since he has my family, they'll disappear anyway."

"No," Saluso said sharply. "Mr. Murphy will know that he cannot hide your family from me. My people will locate them surely in days, perhaps hours. I promise you I have no plans to act against this man until your wife and children are safe."

"Safe in your custody? So now I have to decide which of you two would kill my family most humanely." He didn't answer. "I'm not going to consider this without getting some facts," I said, "and if I hear even one indication that you're hiding something, you can kiss your plan good-bye."

"No, Ben," he said. "I will tell you nothing more until I

receive your guarantee that you will do whatever I ask of you."

"Forget it."

"Do you not understand the consequence of refusing me? There is no choice."

"What if you ask me to kill for you? An assassin's bullet for good old Sid."

"Please," he said, "we are not barbarians here. You have seen that my desire is for the best for my people. Killing Mr. Murphy has never entered my mind."

"I'll bet. So why won't you tell me what your scheme is?" He didn't answer. "You think you've got all the power here, but I do have a choice, Songo."

"What is that?"

"I can throw myself on the mercy of God. I can pray for help and turn you down flat."

"Do you have sufficient faith for that?"

"How much faith would I need? From what I can see, you're going to eliminate all of us whether I help you or not."

"Untrue," he said.

"Oh, but it is true! You've made very sure that no one knows where I am except your own people. All the easier to disappear me when we've served our purpose. My family, wherever they are, can get swallowed up in the coup."

"Many people know you are with me. We visited my village, if you will remember."

"Then why did you stuff me in a car trunk?"

"I have certain enemies since the past election, and I feared they might stop my car. It would be difficult to explain your presence."

"They could have searched your car and found me anyway. Besides, I'd only come to help you plan an election campaign. No, I think you did it to soften me up, to get me to believe that you had me on a short leash."

"Think what you will."

"In any case, I'm sure you can find a nice hole to drop us in after I've done your little job."

"I swear to you, Ben, that if you help me, no harm will come to you or your family."

"Don't swear to me, Songo."

"Do I have your support?"

"Not even halfway. What do you want me to do for you?"

"Whatever I ask."

"Not murder?"

"Not murder."

"I have to think," I said. "Get out of here and let me get my head together." He left without a word.

I paced the room, trying to force my mind to arrange the information I had into an answer. Nothing reassuring came to me.

One way to solve it would have been to tell myself, "Sure you might end up doing something terrible for him, but he hasn't given you any choice."

But he had given me a choice. If Saluso really believed he had me cold, why had he refused to tell me anything about his plan? He had nothing to lose from revealing all unless he knew there was a possibility I'd turn him down. Suppose I did that and it turned out Saluso had only been bluffing about his threat to our lives. In that case, it would make sense that he didn't want me to know very much. He could let us leave the country, and I'd have nothing much to tell the world except that Saluso hadn't treated me very well.

Why else had he been so coy? A quirk in his personality? A love of domination? Maybe.

So there was at least an outside chance that Saluso didn't have the nerve to kill us and that he'd let us go if I refused to help him. But then Murphy still had my family. Did Saluso really have a way of finding them?

I got up and walked to the front window. Outside, beyond the air-conditioning and the wall around the property, Africa still steamed, scarcely cooled by the first rains of the wet season. Out there I knew were millions of people, citizens of the country but all pawns of the few with enough money and guns to hold power. Neither altruism nor even wisdom to govern were part of the equation. Instead, it was that old perversion of the golden rule: He who has the most gold rules.

There's a lot of pious talk that floats around Christian circles about "turning it over to the Lord" and "resting in the Almighty." I could have done what my convictions were shouting at me to do and defied Saluso. But I couldn't tell whether or not he was bluffing.

When in doubt...trust God? Trust yourself? If I refused Saluso, the answer to my doubts would be quick, whatever it was, and it would be out of my control. If I gave in to him, there was a slim chance I could find a way to escape Mtobe with my family.

I might have taken longer, prayed and agonized over it, but I knew then what my decision would be. So I went to the door and called the governor in.

"Songo," I said, "looks like you've got yourself a hired man."

Saluso, a faint smile on his face, stared in rapt admiration at me, his new pet. He must have marveled that Christmas had come early.

"One more thing," I said. "I want my family located and out of the country."

"I can perhaps free them from Mr. Murphy," he said, "but they must remain here in my home."

"No way. My family will not be pawns in this. Do you understand me?"

"I have the understanding that every man has his limits. But if I rescue your family and send them home to America, how can I know that you will do my bidding?"

"Oh that makes a lot of sense," I said. "I'm going to bolt out of your clutches, pass unnoticed in a sea of black faces, and get through some border post without taking a single bullet on the way."

"Sarcasm can be overly harsh, Ben," he said softly.

"And talk is cheap, Saluso. Your assurances mean nothing to me."

"If you are truly a follower of the Master, why can you not trust a fellow believer?"

"You?"

"My drifting from the fervent faith of my spiritual father may be a difficulty for me, but I have never abandoned the Christ. We should be treating each other as brothers."

"In what ways have you drifted?" I asked. "You seem in

every way to be a holy man. Except for your ethics, and who needs ethics anyway?"

"I have made many mistakes, Ben," he said. "I never should have been the friend of Mr. Murphy, and but for the welfare of my people, I would not be associating with such a man."

"Both of us have a puzzle to solve, then, don't we. I've been trying to figure out what I'd be willing to do to save my family. All you have to do is determine how many bodies you're willing to walk over on your way to the throne."

He turned his face quickly to stare out the window. The view was meager from the first floor—only the drab courtyard with its broken-glass tipped wall. I had a far better view from my bedroom.

But could I actually see farther than Saluso did? What did he mean when he told me his sole motivation was the welfare of his people? I'd grown tired over the years of politicians who played the role of Messiah. No matter how lofty their motives, ultimately they ended up serving their own cravings for power.

Now I was going to work for one because I'd convinced myself that the stakes were too high to leave my fate in the hands of God. Rain had started falling outside, and I shivered at the sudden chill.

CHAPTER SEVEN

BEN

The engine coughed, excused itself, and started again, and I suddenly remembered why I hate small planes. Picture a one-engine four-seater, British. I forget the brand. In a car, losing the engine means you call the auto club. In a plane...

The take-off had been hedged in security. Early departure by car from Saluso's palace—long before dawn—me wearing a broad hat and sunglasses to cut down the amount of skin showing. Hurried loading into a plane parked in a far corner of the airport near Saluso's state capital.

I'd tried other means before risking my life in the skies, believe me. The first had been to urge Saluso to let me go directly to the oil companies. You can guess the routine: "Look, people, Murphy's an opportunist who wants to be king. He's all set to take over the country and sell you down the river. Saluso's safer. He'll give you everything you want."

But the governor was adamant. Some proverb to the effect that only a fool plays with a hungry lion. The oil people were devious men who were likely not to believe me. They'd laugh at me and throw me out, then tell Murphy about my interference and my family would be even more at risk. The way Saluso explained it, Murphy had promised the oil people the total security they needed to flourish and grow. They weren't likely to appreciate someone coming out of the blue and suggesting that their golden boy was planning to turn against them.

"You will never be convincing them, Ben," Saluso said. "They're as hungry as Mr. Murphy is."

Plan B. Go to Murphy and tell him that we don't like his nasty scheme. Since the Mtobeans would never tolerate a white man ruling them, he needs Saluso as his front man. But Saluso has decided not to cooperate, so Murphy might as well call off the coup and turn his efforts to helping Saluso win the next election. Maybe Saluso will find a job for him somewhere.

Saluso turned down Plan B too. Murphy was too dangerous. In fact, my old pal Sid was just as likely to have Saluso assassinated and then try his luck with some other African. Saluso made it clear that Murphy, through his bribes and promises, controlled most of the power in the state one way or another.

"We must needs be more careful than that, Ben," Saluso told me. "Your help to rid me of Mr. Murphy must not put me at risk."

"How am I supposed to accomplish that, Songo?" He looked stung at my use of his first name. "Pop into the nearest phone booth and put on my spy uniform? Turn into an African James Bond?"

"Your humor is becoming a pain in my bones," he said, his face sad.

I felt guilty for two seconds. By then, he'd launched into his plan.

"Are you insane?" I asked finally, hearing what he was telling me but not believing anyone would ever suggest such a thing.

"There is much risk, but we are Africans, Ben. We are loud and seem to be without cares, only until it comes time to know who our friends are. Then we have no equals."

That's why I was in a small plane with no government markings, flying to a military base seventy miles northeast of Saluso's headquarters. The papers in my briefcase identified me as one Gordon Duncan, a representative of the U.S. State Department. The papers were very good. Saluso must have paid a fortune for them.

Once I got over my rickety air transport, I began pondering the new information Saluso's plan had given me. Clearly, he'd been working on this scheme for months. You don't forge State Department documents overnight.

Murphy, in securing me as advisor to the governor, had convinced Saluso I was the kind of guy who'd be delighted to blueprint a coup if the money was right. The only thing was, Murphy wanted a coup, but Saluso didn't. That was why I was riding in Saluso's plane all set to play out Saluso's game and probably end up with a bullet in the head for my efforts.

The plane banked suddenly and began following a wide river. Other than the occasional village, the view was all green palms and jungle bush below us. Far to the south, I could see the ocean shoreline, but we were heading inland.

It was time to start rehearsing it—the scheme Saluso had hatched to get out from under Murphy's thumb and supposedly prevent the coup.

Several months before, Murphy and Saluso had co-opted three generals of the Mtobean army who'd agreed to carry out a coup funded through Murphy. Each general led an army base, one northeast of Saluso's state capital, one northwest, and one southwest down near the national capital.

The generals knew that oil money was involved and that Murphy would be pulling a lot of economic strings in Mtobe once Saluso was set up as president. The military, in turn, would have almost total political power as long as they let Murphy nationalize the oil companies and skim off ten percent of the profits. I wondered where they'd sell their oil when the world saw the way they operated, but that wasn't my worry.

I was Gordon Duncan from the State Department. My people in America wanted key elements in Mtobe, particularly the powerful ones such as the army, to be aware that the U.S. of A. was not happy with the current Mtobean government. Nor were we comfortable with the increasing militancy of the oil companies.

The way we saw it, Mtobe needed a major shift to make it a player in the new world economy. The current president was old-fashioned and heavy-handed, especially in his exploitative taxation. On the other hand, the oil companies had enlisted a champion who was not an African—a certain Sid Murphy. Should Sid gain national power, good honest Americans who had fought for civil rights in their own land would see Mtobe turning into a new colonial slave state ruled by a white American, and they wouldn't be happy. Murphy had no business holding power in a proud black African nation. (Advice: Lay it on thick at this point.)

I was supposed to impress the three generals who controlled the armed forces in the three most significant states in the country that, as far as the State Department was concerned, Murphy was out but Saluso was still in. We Americans were fully prepared to support Saluso any way we could, but not as long as Sid Murphy and the oil companies were calling the shots.

Of course, the one obvious problem with the scheme was that it took more than pretty good documents to convince an African general that I was really from the State Department. A few phone calls would reveal that there was no State Department employee named Gordon Duncan, let alone one authorized to contact generals in Mtobe.

But Saluso assured me there was no problem. If someone made a background check, it would reveal that Gordon Duncan was a fully accredited servant of the U.S. government and that he had arrived in Mtobe the day before yesterday. Thanks to a contest Saluso had rigged, the man thought he'd won a two-week vacation in Mtobe. The State Department itself wouldn't have a clue that Duncan was doing anything more than catching some much needed R & R.

In other words, Saluso's plan was running on two cylinders, and I'd be in some stinking dungeon before the week was out. "You are a diplomat, Ben," Saluso had told me confidently.

"Use your charm. Convince these men that you are genuine and that no good will come to them unless they abandon Mr. Murphy and join with me alone."

"So you can carry out a coup yourself?" I asked him.

His look turned to outrage. "I have not ever been interested in a coup, Ben. Mr. Murphy has many desires for a coup, not me. But you must understand that these generals need an allegiance to someone, if not to Mr. Murphy then it must needs be to me."

"What about the duly elected federal government?"

"The military will not give support to this so-called president. They are waiting for someone of strength to lead them. Of course, I am the only logical choice because I am the only one content to wait until it is time to campaign for the presidency yet again. Without a coup."

And so there I was, floating on a wing and a prayer—no, forget the prayer. This was Ben Sylvester flying on his own again. You fool, I told myself. Saluso's probably as bad as Murphy, despite all his assurances. Why are you helping him? Is your family your only reason, or is this little man getting to you?

Well, what if he was genuine? What if he did have an unselfish agenda based solely on love for his country? The people in his home village adored him. His spiritual father, Reverend Craven, told me to trust him. Saluso was a believer—at least he claimed to be—in the same Master as my own.

Maybe my gut feeling that he was slime was based on too much experience with bad apples all around the world. Saluso might be different. Sid Murphy was no prize catch, and if

Saluso really wanted to cut ties with him, then little Songo might just be the genuine article—a man for the people, a hero in the making. Or maybe my guilty mind was just trying to justify what I was about to do.

The plane coughed again and took much longer this time to start sounding like a reliable bet once more. I turned my head to the pilot, who looked back with a grin and said, "Water in the petrol. It is not unusual." He was a bright-eyed young man, intelligent looking, African. Name of Kdoma. Saluso told me he'd just come in from the coast.

"Is there anything I can explain to you, Mr. Sylvester?" Kdoma said.

"Are we going to crash?"

"No, sir. In fact, we will be arriving in fifteen minutes."

"Could we land on that riverbed down there if the engine went out?"

He grinned and turned back to his flying. I guess he couldn't believe I was serious. I should have been praying, but I couldn't put the words together.

Below, the river widened into something like a lake, on one side a sizable village and on the other an airstrip and a large army base, its huts carefully arranged in rows. I could see several groups marching on the parade ground south of the buildings.

That was when the reality hit me, and I heard my stomach rumbling, a somber organ recital to accompany the confused notes in my mind. This would never work. We'd be sent packing or be locked up before we got ten steps out of the plane.

I almost told Kdoma to turn around, but I wasn't sure what his instructions were from Saluso. For all I knew, he had a pistol ready to point at me so that I'd have to go through with it anyway.

We landed on the impossibly narrow paved strip running up the clearing like a ribbon of black tape on a brown floor. Despite all my fears, Kdoma was a great pilot. Not only did we stay on the strip, but there was scarcely a bump before the plane pulled to a halt and shut down.

Instantly we were surrounded by soldiers with guns. I'd expected that. While the airport was under civil control, it was too close to the army base to escape the military having a finger in the pie. The moment I got off, there were loud voices all around me—"Who are you? What are you doing here? Where is your authorization?"

Though I'd been prepared for it, there's something about guns in your face and shouting soldiers that forces out the adrenaline and gets the heart racing. To show them I meant no harm, I sat on the step leading out of the plane, stared at the ground and waited.

The most senior of the soldiers, a large graying man with sergeant's stripes highlighting a standard dark green uniform, approached and held out his hand. "Your authorization, please."

"I wish to see the general in charge."

He laughed, real mirth in his voice. "Do you think your white face has power here? How did you think you could come here without authorization?"

I reached into my shirt and pulled out a small identification wallet, the State Department insignia bold on the card inside it. His eyes widened.

I was burning with shame over the charade I was playing, wishing I could call it off, wishing God would come in and solve the whole thing for me, knowing that I'd chosen for him not to.

The sergeant brought me to a colonel, who frowned and tisked and made it clear he had no idea what to do with me. This was not the way a foreign power did business with the armed forces of Mtobe. Finally, after leaving me to cool my heels in an air-conditioned officers' lounge, shabby but clean, he led me to headquarters.

The general's office was luxurious by army standards, more like a boardroom in a mid-level company in the States. The head honcho himself sat behind a luminous desk which was totally clear except for a pen set and a notepad.

"Mr. Duncan," he said, "you have thrown my staff into confusion." He was a small man, chubby, with thick glasses, dark rims. I guessed him to be about sixty. His voice was deep, his accent tinged with British culture.

"I'm sorry for that, general," I said, trying to look confident and official. "With the kind of mission I'm on, it wasn't advisable to pre-arrange my arrival."

"We are a sovereign country, in case you have not been made aware of that fact. The United States State Department has not received any jurisdiction here."

"Nor do we want any, general," I said. "I am here merely to share with you some mutual concerns our two nations must deal with. My visit is secret. In fact, my superiors would disavow all knowledge of my work here should anyone ask." I hoped the *Mission: Impossible* TV series had never been shown in Mtobe.

"Please, Mr. Duncan," the general said, waving his hand. "Let's not be having any of this cloak-and-dagger nonsense here. You are carrying a message for me. Tell me what it is."

"We're concerned about the growing rift between your federal government and the oil companies. As you know, Mtobe supplies much of our oil imports and has an important seat on O.P.E.C."

"You believe Mtobe is mismanaging its oil interests?"

"It doesn't matter what I believe. The oil companies are screaming about over-taxation and loss of revenue mainly due to the incompetence of your president. What's more, they're looking for a champion, and they're not above financing a coup if the situation gets bad enough."

"Come now, Mr. Duncan."

"It is our understanding that the oil companies are funding a certain Sidney Murphy, an American, and he has approached you in the company of Governor Saluso to win your support for a coup."

I suppose I didn't actually hear a thunderclap at that moment, but I'll always remember it that way. The little general erupted with fury and shouts that would have sent any real storm cowering with its tail between its legs.

"How dare you come here unannounced and without proper authorization to accuse me of conspiring with enemies of my government. I am a loyal servant of the president..." and so on.

I waited for him to cool down, but it was fifteen minutes before he stopped. I heard his life story as well as a precise statement of the relationship between the duly elected government and the armed forces of Mtobe. Finally there was heavy silence as he caught his breath.

I opened the briefcase and pulled out the documents, beginning with a letter from one oil executive to another, on oil company letterhead, detailing Sid Murphy's mandate to organize a coup and listing three generals by name as co-conspirators.

Along with it, as counterfeit as the letter, was a photocopy of a U.S. government report stamped top secret. I'd read it carefully, and I had to admit it was well done—a comprehensive analysis of the political situation in Mtobe, again naming Murphy and three generals by name as co-conspirators in a planned coup, with a strong recommendation that the U.S. oppose the oil companies and put all its eggs in Songo Saluso's basket.

Saluso was shown to be a puppet of Murphy, yet he had potential to win the presidency legitimately if only Murphy were out of the picture. To bring that about, the State Department was prepared to release to the news media a full report on the coup conspiracy, naming names.

I let the general read in silence. When he looked up, the fire in his eyes had been snuffed out and was barely smoking. He stared at me as if I were holding a battle-ax over his head.

"We want you to change your allegiance, general," I said. "Tell Murphy the coup he wants is off and that you'll have nothing to do with him or the oil companies ever again. If

Governor Saluso wants your help for anything, he'll contact you and you'll do it. And I do mean anything."

Saluso had insisted on this last instruction even though my words could open the door for him to go to the generals and arrange for his own coup without Murphy.

"All right," said the general, making a little gesture of defeat and putting his head in his hands. "I will do what you have ordered."

It was too easy.

CHAPTER EIGHT

KAREN

Karen savored the domestic clatter of Kelly Smithers going cheerfully about the endless task of keeping a large house in the African bush. It was one of the few positive memories she could take with her from their African adventure. If they hadn't been confined to the house and if she hadn't been so burdened by her fears for Ben, she could have enjoyed this kind of life almost as much as the vacation they had lost.

But whenever she remembered that it had been Sid Murphy who had brought them there, she felt fear for the safety of her children. There were only two reasons why she'd agreed to stay with the Smithers: it seemed safer there than anywhere else she could think of, and she trusted Tom and Kelly.

Karen and her children were hiding from the governor for Ben's safety as much as for their own. If there was any reason to believe they were available to be hostages, Ben could be forced to do whatever Governor Saluso wanted him to do. At least, that's what Sid told Karen.

She actually believed Sid for awhile, until they got themselves loaded into the car at the hotel and maybe even an hour more. Perhaps she would have believed him even longer—the man had such a cunning way of covering over the dishonesty that controlled his life. But as he sat across from her and the children in the limousine, he began to look shifty. It wasn't anything overt like a blush or a twitch, but his manner made it clear to Karen that he hadn't told her the whole truth.

"Are you sure we have to move?" she asked him. "Ben is expecting us to stay at your hotel."

"I've already explained that to you," he said. "Governor Saluso is too close to us. You saw how his soldiers could have swooped down on us at any time. If I put you where Saluso can't find you, Ben won't have to cooperate with him."

"You'll make sure that Ben is contacted? To tell him that we're safe, I mean, so he won't have to do anything that isn't right."

"Of course," he said. That was the exact moment she knew for sure Sid had been lying to her. The flicker of his eye, the slight catch in his voice, and the way he folded his hands on his lap all spoke the truth to her.

Her head started to ache, but she tried to smile to let Sid think she believed what he'd said. Inside, though, she was angry and fearful that she'd listened to him and let him put her innocent children into more possible danger. What were they going to do? Why was God so silent?

It was a long journey—at least six hours. The car was a different limousine this time. Karen supposed that the last one needed a lot of repairs after all the damage from the bullets.

Jack and Jimmie never seemed to have their fill of Africa, and they spent their time looking at the farms and villages perched in the jungle and at the school children that flocked all over the road among the goats and chickens and assorted traders.

Karen would have been excited by the sights herself if it hadn't been for her fears for Ben. She couldn't bear the possibility that an evil man might try to force him to do things that would put his life in danger. He was too young in his faith to be facing this kind of challenge. She knew how close to suicide he had been, and she never wanted to fear for him that way again.

Sid Murphy sat on the seat opposite them, saying nothing after their first discussion. He was dressed in his normal blue jeans, but now he wore a loud Hawaiian shirt. The horn, as usual, honked constantly, jarring Karen's nerves.

Not surprisingly, she found that she was turning inward and starting to build a shell the way she used to as a child when her father hurt her with one of his tirades. It was terribly frustrating that she still had so much of a problem dealing properly with her stress. With effort, she escaped the mental snare she was making for herself and started to pray like she never had before.

They stopped only for bathroom breaks, humiliating episodes in the bush. They ate sandwiches while they traveled, going steadily eastward, with the coast somewhere on their right, maybe thirty miles away. She tried to memorize the route they were taking, but there were no road signs on the highway, and most of the towns they drove through had names that were impossible for her to remember. With God so silent now, seemingly so unwilling to help them, she started to wonder if she was losing her hold on reality.

Finally, later in the afternoon, they reached their destination, which to Karen looked like just another town. Going beyond the heavily populated core, where the market was, they drove a couple of miles to a large house in a compound of about an acre, surrounded by a cement wall about chest high.

"Where are we?" she asked.

"You'll be safe here," Murphy said.

"Is this some sort of prison?"

Sid Murphy laughed. "It's no prison, and you're not prisoners. Some missionaries live here. They've agreed to take you in."

They drove past a big steel gate up to a wide, low house with a large patio in front of the main doors. The house might not have been called a mansion by most people's standards, but it was huge. It looked quite old and was made of cement blocks that had been painted pale blue. From what Karen could see of it, there wasn't any glass in the windows, only shutters opened to reveal heavy crisscrossed wires where glass might have been. The double front doors were wide open.

Jack and Jimmie got out with her uncertainly, hanging back. No one could blame them; Karen's heart was beating fast too. She had no real idea where they were or how they could reach Ben or how they could get back to the States—all of them, Ben included.

Then Kelly Smithers, the missionary, came out on the

patio. She was in her early thirties and dressed in a flowery cotton skirt and mint-green blouse. Her smile spoke of welcome and peace.

"You're Karen Sylvester," she said brightly. "Mr. Murphy sent word to us about you. Don't worry—as far as Tom and I are concerned, you and the kids can stay as long as you want."

Sid Murphy interrupted, speaking to Karen. "I explained to them the trouble you've had. If you can stay a week or so, I'll do my best to send word to Ben and try to get him away from the governor." He saw the doubtful expression on her face. "Look, Karen, Saluso needs me and the oil money. If I tell him Ben is off limits and you're out of his control, he'll have to see reason."

She smiled weakly at Sid and nodded her head. He seemed to have a satisfied look as he got into the car and his driver drove him away.

Once he was gone, Karen turned to Kelly, who was waiting on the steps. The boys were standing behind her, still unsure of themselves.

"Come in," Kelly said. "You're in the territory of mad dogs and Englishmen out there. It's far cooler inside."

They exchanged the usual sorts of pleasantries: "I hope we're not a bother." "No, of course not. We love visitors"—and so on. There was a feeling of warmth there that was wonderful after the coldness of Sid Murphy's hotel. To feel so instantly at home was a luxury Karen could easily have reveled in, but she knew the feeling of safety and security was an illusion. Kelly Smithers was no more able to save them from Saluso or Sid Murphy than Karen was. At the very least, she sensed that Kelly could be trusted, and that was a comfort. This was a woman of faith and of commitment to the same Lord who had given Karen such an abundant new life.

"Tom is still at the college, but he should be back by three," Kelly explained as she led them into the living room. The floor was cement that had been painted a deep burgundy. The chairs and sofa were covered with bright blue cloth in an African design.

"Is your husband expecting us?" Karen asked as she sat down. The boys sat next to her, Jimmie being uncharacteristically quiet and Jack looking as if storm clouds were circling over his head.

"Don't worry about Tom," she said. "He absolutely loves visitors. Look, Mrs. Sylvester—"

"Call me Karen."

"Karen, then. I know you're in the middle of some very difficult problems. Why don't we start out by being open with each other?"

"What has Sid told you about our situation?"

"Not very much. And if we were looking for the truth about something, I don't think Sid Murphy would be a very reliable source for it."

"How do you know him?"

"When we first came out here five years ago, Tom was in the oil business." Kelly sat down on an armchair and settled into it comfortably. "I don't remember exactly how we met Sid. He seemed to spend a lot of time in our town."

"Town?"

"The oil companies like to create whole towns for their

employees. Really they're just walled ghettos to keep the national people out."

"And Murphy was running his hotel then?" Karen asked.

"As far as I know. Someone told us he'd come into some money in South Africa. Diamonds, I think. My feeling is he probably smuggled them out. In any case, even though his hotel was miles away he always seemed to be having meetings with the top executives in our company."

"And he knew them well?" Karen asked. "It wasn't that he was just hanging around?"

"That's how it looked to me—as if he was doing business with them. Is that important?"

"I guess it agrees with some of the things he told me about himself."

"Karen, we need to be open about this. I think you're in serious trouble, and Tom and I want to help."

"I haven't been trying to be secretive. I've been so terrified for the past week that it feels absolutely wonderful to talk to someone who's not being devious. What did Sid tell you about us?"

"He said that Governor Saluso has taken control of your husband and wants to use you and your children as hostages."

Karen looked at Jack, whose expression seemed even darker than it had been when they started their journey. Wheels appeared to be turning in his mind, and she could picture him imagining horrible things again. Jimmie was starting to fidget.

"Is there somewhere the children could play?" she asked hesitantly.

"Down that hallway and to the left," Kelly said. "We've got a bat and ball by the back door. The courtyard out there has a high wall around it so they'll be safe." They got up and introduced the kids to their new ball park. This shouldn't have been their world—filled with greed and violence and deceitful men, Karen thought. God, they shouldn't be experiencing this.

By the time they got back, tea and cookies had appeared, brought in by an African woman about twenty. Kelly introduced Karen to Elizabeth, who worked for the Smithers to support herself and her preschool daughter.

"We want to help you, Karen," Kelly repeated.

"There's really not very much you can do."

"We can hide you from the governor."

"Is that possible? I'm not even sure where we are."

"You're not in Saluso's state anymore." When Kelly explained that the border with the next country was about sixty miles west by road, Karen asked her how far they were from the coast.

"About thirty-five miles," she said. "Are you and your kids hoping to flee the country?"

"Not without Ben."

"There's something else we can do," Kelly said.

"Pray?" Karen sighed, feeling a profound exhaustion.

"Some people don't believe in it."

"Don't worry—I'm a believer just like you."

At that, Kelly brightened considerably. So they prayed, long and earnestly, even though Karen felt as though she could scarcely understand God anymore. Their prayer time ended abruptly when Jimmie burst in saying something about seven chickens in the backyard and a rooster leading them around.

"That's Tyrone," Kelly explained. "He thinks he rules the world. Don't be surprised if he starts crowing under your window at three in the morning. Tom says he'd be more helpful boiling in a pot, but I don't have the heart."

Kelly showed them their rooms—one for the boys and one for Karen—with double beds in each and mosquito nets hanging from the ceiling on bamboo frames. Karen didn't want to be there imposing on them, and yet she savored this refuge in the storm. Maybe they'd be safe for awhile. Only God and Governor Saluso knew how Ben was doing, and neither was telling.

Tom came home about an hour later. A thin scholarly looking man with glasses and thick black hair, he taught at a local Bible school. Once they'd met him, the boys went back to their ballgame. Trying to bury her fears in conversation, Karen asked Tom, over a cup of tea, why he'd left a lucrative career in the oil business to teach on subsistence wages at a Bible school.

"Years ago I got a degree in theology and planned to be a missionary," he said. "But we lost our nerve, so I went back to geology, since I'd majored in it in college."

"And we ended up in Africa," Kelly put in. "Sanitized Africa in a nice little oil company ghetto. I hated it. On the other side of the English country hedges, just beyond the Olympic pool and the ten-foot steel fences, were people living in poverty and despair."

"We started to venture into the real Africa," Tom said, "and my life took on meaning again as we got to know the people. After that we found we just couldn't stay in the ghetto. So when I heard of a mission that needed a Bible school teacher, we dumped the oil career and came here."

Karen felt as if she should have been more attentive to what they were telling her about their lives. These people had carved out a significant purpose for themselves, but she found she couldn't think of anything much but Ben.

"Tom," she asked, "if Sid Murphy is working for the oil companies, could you contact some of your old friends and try to find out what's happening and why our family is involved in it? Maybe someone knows where Ben is."

"Have you heard anything at all from your husband?" he asked.

"No," she said, trying to keep her voice from breaking but not doing very well.

"Is there anything else you need to find out?" he asked softly.

"Probably this will just sound foolish to you," she said, "but I think Sid Murphy and Governor Saluso have been working together all along and only pretending to be at odds with each other. I think they're having their expenses paid by the oil companies to carry out a coup together."

"Do you really think any oil executive is going to admit to me that his company is funding a plot to take over the country?" he asked.

"It was just a thought. If you don't think it will do any good…"

"Don't give up so fast," Tom said. "I'll see what I can do."

"It could be dangerous for you," Karen said.

"Why?"

"There seems to be so much at stake."

"Tomorrow's Saturday," he said. "If I drive over at daylight, I can probably be back by four. All right?" His "all right" was directed to Kelly.

"Sure," she said, but too quickly. It was obvious to Karen that it wasn't all right. Kelly was scared. But Karen couldn't bring herself to tell him not to go.

The kids slept restlessly in their strange bed. They'd been used to air conditioning, not to the heat and humidity of a humble mission house. About three in the morning, they climbed into bed with Karen, and she watched over them, lying awake, until dawn.

She was awake when Tom's VW van pulled out at six-thirty, and she remained watchful while the kids played in the back courtyard all morning. By mid-afternoon, the children had started whining about nothing left to do and wanting to go back to the beach.

Tom got back about four-thirty, looking puzzled and unsure. "What is it?" Kelly asked him as he sat down in the front room.

"They wouldn't tell me anything about Murphy or Saluso," he said. "Not even Craig would talk about them."

"You were best friends," Kelly said.

"I think Craig thought his office was bugged," Tom said. "He spent the whole time diverting us into conversation about the old days. When I mentioned Murphy's name, he shook his head and changed the subject. Just as he said good-bye, he gave me this."

Tom handed a note, hesitantly, to Kelly. She read it, and her face filled with sudden confusion. Then she passed it over to Karen. The note said:

Take Kelly and get out of the country. Do it fast. Tomorrow morning at the latest.

CHAPTER NINE

BEN

T wo hours," Kdoma said, giving me a pitying look as I boarded the plane after asking, "How long is the trip this time?" My relationship with planes, bad already, was deteriorating rapidly.

We flew northwest, the familiar terrain of jungle, river, and farms shifting gradually toward grassland. The second army base we were flying to was just outside Saluso's state, forming a triangle with the one I'd just left and the third base south of it. If I actually survived this second trip, I still had a third one to look forward to that would take me right next to the national capital, a prospect I still wasn't ready to think about.

We flew along for an hour or so before Kdoma spoke again, shouting over the engine noise. "Mr. Sylvester, why are you doing this?"

"Doing what?" I asked.

"It's obvious to me that you are serving as the governor's emissary. These are national army bases we are going to. State governors should not be making schemes with federal generals."

"Who said anything about schemes?" I shouted back at him.

"We have some things in common," Kdoma said. "Both of us are followers of the Way."

"Excuse me?"

"We are Christians. Servers of Jesus Christ."

"How did you know that?"

"I have means of knowing such things. Why then, Mr. Sylvester, do you think it proper to lie to a brother in the Lord?"

"Circumstances," I said. "Sometimes there are no choices."

"You are being forced to do wrong?"

"What option do I have?"

"Faith. Trust in God."

"I don't see any giant hands reaching out of the sky to pluck me out of this situation."

"Our God does not work in that way."

"I know he doesn't."

"Is your way better? Wiser?" he asked. "Can you do what God cannot?"

"Your job is to fly the plane," I told him. "So fly it."

We flew on, the awkward silence drowned out by the noise of the engine. There was no way I wanted to let on to him what a sensitive nerve he'd struck. Kdoma was dead on—I was a fool to be serving as willing slave for some half-baked little wanna-be potentate. In the process it was clear that I was losing everything—self-respect, faith, God, all of it left somewhere behind in Saluso's palace when I made the decision to play his game. The irony of it was that I couldn't be sure that anything I did would save Karen and my boys anyway.

"Are you there?" I said softly, Kdoma unable to hear me. But he was gone, this God who had saved me from despair, maybe suicide. I'd taken the only one who had ever offered me real life, and then when I had a chance to trust him, I'd cast him aside and gone back to living by my wits.

The more I studied Saluso's scheme, the more I realized he'd crafted it so any competent American with some political smarts could have played my role. He hadn't even bothered to create a picture ID. If I'd turned Saluso down, I was reasonably sure he would have let me go. Maybe he even had an alternate waiting somewhere in the wings.

Now I was in the middle of something far dirtier than it looked. Saluso wasn't just getting rid of Murphy. He was frightening the rebellious generals right into his pocket. If the Americans ever released my documents to the press, it would mean a quick execution for any general involved. The generals would do exactly what Saluso ordered as long as they knew the Americans were backing him.

It wasn't worth it. The realization came suddenly just as we moved into landing position. It wasn't worth it selling out to Saluso, no matter what they—

"Your seat belt," Kdoma shouted. "Is it made tight?"

"Yes," I shouted back.

"Turbulence. Make yourself ready."

We bounced hard in the unstable air, the vibrations getting worse the closer we got to the ground. An air pocket dropped us a good thirty feet, and I felt my breakfast coming back to say hello. Then finally, far too much later, we connected with the runway, safe and intact.

There was the expected noise and confusion at the air base. Just like before, I showed my false IDs and the soldiers ushered me in to see the general.

This one was more of a scholar type, dignified and inquisitive, and he scared me from the first. I went through my routine, showing him the false State Department documents, then the letter linking him and the other two generals to the oil companies and Murphy. He absorbed everything, reading it slowly, asking me questions I was hard-pressed to answer so that I had to expand on my story as I went along.

Then suddenly he folded, just like the first guy, clutching a copy of the incriminating letter, staring at me as if I could save him if only I'd keep quiet about his nasty little secret. I watched him in silence, not thinking about anything, just wallowing in the guy's misery along with him.

"Mr. Duncan?"

I shuddered, breaking free from the numbness seeping into my brain like a drug.

"General?"

"What can I do now?" he asked. "How can I correct my error?"

This was my cue to tell him to cut all his ties with Murphy and align himself with Saluso. But I couldn't speak—the words were lost down some dark valley where I couldn't reach them. It wasn't possible to speak them, and I knew it never would be possible again.

"May I have that?" I asked, my voice raspy. I reached for the forged letter he was holding and pulled it roughly out of his hand. For a second I stared at it, knowing its power, feeling its inherent evil. Then I ripped the letter in half. My hands seemed to work on their own, without guiding thought, grabbing the false documents off the general's desk, ripping them up.

I can explain it now. If you asked me, I would tell you that I'd come to the end of trying to justify Saluso's dirty scheme and my part in it. My survival, even my family's survival, really wasn't in my hands. Saluso could as easily have killed us after I cooperated as he could have if I'd refused him.

So far I hadn't found an escape hatch, and I doubted I ever would. Meanwhile I'd tossed aside the only One who could help me, and I'd put traitorous generals right into Saluso's pocket. It was time to cut bait.

That's maybe my explanation now. When I did it, I'm not sure I knew what my reason was except that I couldn't endure this another minute.

The general was flabbergasted. He kept trying to pull the documents back, but I was too fast for him, my hands ripping and tearing. Finally, we stared at each other, both of us too shocked for words. When he spoke, it was the obvious question.

"I'm a fraud, General," I told him. "Everything I told you is a lie, all of it. Total fabrication."

"Who are you then?"

"Nobody. Just somebody's slave. Governor Saluso set it all up for me."

"You are not from the State Department?"

"No. And these papers are worth absolutely nothing. They're all forgeries."

"You would have succeeded."

"I know." When he called in his men, I wouldn't have been surprised if he'd just had me hauled out back and shot.

"Put him under guard for now," he said, "but do not harm him."

The squad of soldiers took me to a cell stuck on the end of a barracks, something probably used for personnel who stepped out of line. Right then, thankfully, it was empty, a bleak room, maybe ten by twelve.

Cement floor, cement block walls, metal bed with two-inch mattress, basic latrine equipment on the floor in one corner, a basin with water in another, no other furniture. The door was steel, with a lockable feeding slot. The ceiling was made of heavy timbers, and I'd seen a metal roof over the room before they dragged me into the cell. There was only one window facing out onto an alley between the cell and the next barracks. The bars were just like those in a 1950s western, and I half expected Roy Rogers to ride up, throw a rope around a couple of them, and use Trigger to yank them out.

Alone, totally alone with darkness falling and the lights inside me going out one by one. If God would have been listening, I would have prayed, but I'd shoved him away and had no idea where he was.

Can you understand the terror I felt, alone, cursed, with the night coming on fast and maybe a firing squad getting ready for the morning?

My family. There was probably nothing for them now. Saluso could track them down, and they'd disappear. I hoped—almost prayed—that there wouldn't be any pain. No doubt there was an extra curse in hell for a man who sold out his family.

Stupid. Stupid Ben Sylvester, I told myself, realizing it was childish, but unable to stop myself. You will never get it right, no matter how many hours you live.

The hardest part was wondering where God had gone. I'd started out in some sort of awkward dance with him, never sure whether I'd step on his toes or we'd glide across the floor in harmonious poetry. But half the time lately we weren't waltzing; we were wrestlers crouched to grapple, eyeballing one another, wondering who would take the advantage and assert his power.

Now he was gone again, shoved aside, and with darkness clutching at me, I was utterly unable to face the prospect of the night. In the morning I'd probably die, and no one who loved me would ever know what had happened to me.

"Are you there?" I must have said it. It was my voice and God knew no one else was in the cell. My voice calling out to someone long gone, left behind when I defied him and joined ranks with Governor Saluso. Stupid Ben Sylvester, calling out to God now that he couldn't save himself. Why did you agree to this whole deception if you really trusted God? Did you really think you'd do better than he could?

I'd tried to convince myself all along that I didn't have any choice. But I knew better. The only reason I'd given in to Saluso was that it gave me time to think of some way to escape him. I didn't want to refuse the man because that would have left my fate with God. And my fate was too important to me to let it out of my own hands.

I'd expected the night to be total darkness, but instead the cell window let in the glare of a floodlight about thirty yards away. A couple of hours after the sun went down, the soldier sounds ended, and there was silence except for one sentry who passed the window every half hour or so.

I longed for Karen, just to hold her, get some strength from her. I didn't want to go out alone. Not even the crummy sentry would look at me.

They'd probably do it with a single shot to the back of the head. Firing squads were out of date, too banana-republic. One second to pass from full living consciousness to a hunk of meat hitting the ground, soul flying who knew where.

In the darkness, a chopper suddenly flew in low from the south, lights glaring into my cell, beating me back to a gloomier corner. The noise died. Voices far away. Then silence again. I would have been happy for a ticking clock or a dripping faucet. I started to look forward to the few seconds it took the sentry to pass, the only relief I had to the frightening monotony of my last hours.

Dawn was lighting the air above the jungle before I heard myself saying again, "Are you there?"

If he spoke to me, I didn't hear it.

CHAPTER TEN

BEN

The cell door opened suddenly, the lock snapping back, hinges shrieking. I jerked awake. Somehow in the last hour of the night, I must have fallen asleep. Saluso was standing there in some kind of military uniform. He looked somber, hurt dignity written all over his face.

Groggy, I sat up, then stood in front of him, hoping my height advantage would do me some good.

"Is my family safe?" I blurted, condemning myself for revealing the ache inside me, the weakness Saluso might still use against me.

"Your family does not matter at this time, Ben." His voice was thin, weary.

"Is this when you tell me how disappointed you are in my behavior?"

"I thought you understood my vision. Do you always betray those who are trusting you?"

"I never gave you the slightest reason to trust me, Songo."

"You have presented me with serious difficulties," he said, his face tense. "Ben, this has become a very complicated problem. I—"

He didn't finish. Someone was being let into the cell, and when I saw him, I began to have trouble breathing. I'd been conned. I wondered how I'd managed to get everything so completely wrong.

"Hey, Ben." It was Sid Murphy, looking as scruffy as ever, a smirk on his face. He went over and stood beside Saluso, as if he feared I'd pound him into the ground. I thought about it, believe me. The two of them stood together, smug buddies, the big man and the little man, both of them stuffed to the eyelids with treachery.

"At least you've been clever about it," I said. Saluso looked uncomfortable. Murphy had apparently decided to stay with smug. "Let me see if I've got this right," I went on. "There never was any conflict between you two, was there?"

"No," Saluso said.

Murphy turned on him. "We don't need to explain anything to this idiot."

"You still need me, Mr. Murphy," Saluso told him sharply. "Do not ever forget that."

"Is the second honeymoon over so soon?" I asked.

"Have you no understanding that your life is at great risk here?" Saluso said to me, anger making his voice quaver. "I am willing to offer an explanation to you if only you will stop speaking long enough for me to present it."

"So explain."

For a few seconds he hesitated, obviously trying to determine how to put the best face on treachery.

"The State Department—"

"Shut up, Songo," Murphy said. "He doesn't need to know."

"The State Department of the United States," Saluso went on, "had learned that Mr. Murphy and I were hoping to come into control of the government of my nation by force, using money which came from leaders in the oil companies. The Americans were aware of Mr. Murphy's work in this, but they failed to understand my role."

"For God's sake, shut up," Murphy said.

"Leave God out of this," I told him.

"Could you truly believe," Saluso said, "that black generals in a black African country would be selling themselves to Western oil companies through the intervention of a white man?"

"So you were to be the coup leader all along."

"It was my vision that inspired the generals. Mr. Murphy has supplied only the money and your name."

"So why did you need me?"

"It was possible, I suppose, to find some derelict American within Mtobe and pay him to help us. But these generals are well educated and astute. We wanted a Gordon Duncan who knew how to answer questions of politics with great skill. The generals had to be convinced that they were dealing with the American government."

"And what about the militaristic youth organization Murphy supposedly leads?"

"I permitted him control of the Young Pioneers to

impress the oil men that Mr. Murphy had true responsibility. In fact, these pioneers had been never more than a few hundred exuberant young people."

"You put a contingent of them outside your own home village. Your beloved Reverend Craven is terrified of them."

"He is my father, the one who cared for me as a child. I could not face him if he believed I had involvement in planning an insurrection. The presence of the Youth Corps was convincing him that Mr. Murphy was the one who planned the insurrection."

"What's he going to believe after the coup?"

"It will be necessary to demonstrate to him that I learned of the insurrection only in its final stagings, and I must put myself forward to be compromise leader in order to avoid further bloodshed."

"And the oil companies will get all kinds of perks as rewards for their help," I added. "So why did you need me really?"

"I have already explained. We knew that the generals must believe that Mr. Murphy was no longer to be involved. If they believed that you were truly from the State Department, they would do what you told them to do."

"Was this Songo's idea?" I asked Sid. He didn't answer. "Talk to me, Murphy! You owe me something." He glared at me.

"We both knew of the problem," Saluso said. "I suggested this deception as a way to convince the Americans that Mr. Murphy no longer had any influence to lead a coup."

"I thought you were smarter than that, Sid," I said.

"What a stupid contrived scheme you bought into. Don't you understand that the only thing Songo wanted was to take the control of the generals away from you?"

"Of course I thought of that," he said. "But he needed the financial backing of the oil companies and that meant he couldn't dump me."

"Did you know he was going to nationalize the oil companies?"

"What?" Interesting reaction to my stab in the dark.

"He was scamming you. He really wanted you out of the scene."

"No, he didn't."

"No, I did not," Saluso said.

"That's the problem, isn't it?" I said. "The two of you are so deep into deception that no one can untangle who's conning who."

"I trust him," Murphy said.

"Did I ruin everything?" I asked.

"Would you be in sorrow if you had?" Saluso asked, taking a couple of steps toward me. Murphy hung back, giving me the somber look of a hunter who's just bagged his first deer.

Saluso went on with his explanation. "We needed you. Mr. Murphy assured me that you would have no squeamishness about the ethics of our scheme. Now you have been an embarrassment to us. My generals are feeling betrayed."

"They were," I said. "You used me to lie to your own people."

"Only to convince the generals. If they had believed they

were actually forsaking Mr. Murphy, then whatever spies were among them would believe it too. The Americans would no longer fear that Mr. Murphy and the oil companies had power to lead a coup."

"Did you say spies?"

"Someone in the military has been sending information to the Americans."

"If you've got a spy reporting to the U.S., you've got a spy reporting to your own federal government too."

"Shut up, Ben," Murphy said, his voice even, almost relaxed. "You have no idea what safeguards we've got in place."

"No doubt," I told him. "You guys would put the Three Stooges to shame. So what damage have I done to your nasty little plot?"

"We have three angry generals," Murphy said. "Now they'll have to do some play-acting to convince their officers that they really have dropped me in favor of Songo. If you'd done what you were told to do, they wouldn't have to fake it. But no worries, Ben, it's no big deal."

"No big deal? You risked me and my family for no big deal?"

"I've got money and money buys people."

How in the world did Simpson agree to this? Simpson—our chief of operations. I was already wondering as well why the company hadn't sent any backup to get me out of this mess. Probably they had no way of knowing what black hole I'd dropped into.

"So what's next on my agenda?" I asked.

"A bullet in the head." Murphy said it as if he was joking, but he wasn't. "Them's the breaks, Ben."

"You hate me that much?"

"This isn't personal, just business. Sometimes you have to remove obstacles."

"Mr. Murphy." Saluso. His voice was tense. "I must needs speak with Ben alone."

"No way. You're softening on this, Songo. I'm not going to give him a chance to sweet-talk you into letting him go."

"Must I remind you, Mr. Murphy—" He didn't have to finish the sentence because Sid made a dismissive gesture and walked out without a word. Saluso had more power than I'd suspected.

I stared at Saluso, this man who was such a mix of emotions: excitement, arrogance, fear, uncertainty, everything open to me as I saw him with the clarity of the doomed. Ever since I'd torn up the documents, my vision had been etched with clear silhouettes, light and dark alternating in sharply defined contrasts. If the thoughts about my future, my family, hadn't been so bleak, I might have enjoyed my heightened senses.

"What happened to you, Governor?" I said. "Your Reverend Craven raised you in the faith, and you obviously used to give at least lip service to it. But look at you now."

"What would cause you to believe that God is no longer on my side?"

"The lying, the scheming, the violence—do you want me to go on?"

"Securing justice will at times demand drastic measures."

"If you put that little saying next to Sid's 'Sometimes you have to remove obstacles,' you'd have a poem. Free verse, maybe, but it has a certain—"

"It is too difficult to get used to your sarcasm, Ben." Saluso went over to the window and looked out through the bars.

"Indulge me," I said. "Goodness knows at this stage I don't have many other luxuries left." I walked to the window he was staring out of. "What's so interesting?"

"Nothing. I am trying to..." He paused.

"Yes?"

"This is too difficult for me. You see, I have no desire for you to die."

"So let me go."

"You know too much of this."

"Doris Day and Jimmie Stewart."

"I do not understand your reference." Saluso looked confused.

"*The Man Who Knew Too Much.* Terrific movie."

"Your sense of humor is too unusual. Can you not understand what will soon happen to you?"

"Sid Murphy, my old friend, is going to shoot me in the head." I was locked in an eerie detachment, as if I were watching myself.

"Though you may not believe this, I wish to protect you, Ben. You are not the devious man Mr. Murphy claimed you to be."

"Why would my blood on your hands make any difference? Other people are going to die because of you, maybe lots of them."

"You are a worshipper of God." It took effort for him to get it out.

"I'm the jinx, aren't I, the bad omen. Kill me and maybe God won't help you get your heart's desire."

He was angry. "Why must you insist on making trivial everything I do? I am not a seeker of glory or honor or any such things, only the good of my people."

"You don't get it, do you," I said. "Life isn't a game of chess. I'm not a knight or a bishop or a pawn that you can knock over without a pang. You say you know what's best for the people of your country, but that must mean they've lost their brains. After all, they voted for someone else in the last election, not you. Now you want to force them to accept you."

"I am only regretting," he said, "that we called you to come here. I had many doubts from the beginning."

"What happened to you?" I asked. "You started out with high ideals, and you ended up with Murphy."

"High ideals cannot ever win elections in this place, Ben. Money wins elections—money and power."

"Despite all the money you had, you lost the election anyway, and now you're settling for a coup. How can you possibly think that God could still be on your side?"

He glared at me. "Some causes are justifiable, no matter how much you may need to contradict your scruples."

"Could you answer something for me?" I asked.

"What is it?"

"If I'd turned you down at the beginning, would you have let us go?"

"Yes."

"The truth?"

"I would not have killed you or your family."

"What about Murphy? He would have wanted me dead."

"Mr. Murphy has the false belief that his money provides him with power. It is only when he reminds himself that a white man cannot rule this country that he understands how much more power I have."

"To be his puppet?"

"Do not be so certain of that."

"I was right, wasn't I? You really wanted to cut him off. You wanted to lead your own coup then nationalize the oil."

"Nonsense."

"Is there anything you won't do for power?"

"I will not kill you."

"That's only the jinx. You're afraid that if you kill a believing American, God will get you."

"I am very tired of your unwise speech, Ben," he said. "You do not understand the African."

"I understand that you've abandoned whatever help you could have had from God. If you really wanted to help your people, why did you take this route?"

"Am I to suppose from your words that you have demonstrated perfect trust in God? Do you not understand that I would have let you return to America if you had refused me?"

"How do I know you're telling the truth? Did you have an alternate plan in place?"

"Perhaps. If I did, I certainly would not tell you."

"I had no choice but to go along with this scheme," I said.

"There is always a choice."

"Why didn't you try to raise your funds legitimately?"

"Please do not be naive, Ben."

"So what are you going to do? If you kill me, it might be the last straw. God might decide you're not worth his help anymore, just like you fear."

Silence while Saluso looked at the ceiling as if hoping for inspiration. Finally he spoke.

"I tried, Ben. When I was a child I was wanting so much to embrace the faith of Reverend Craven. But his faith was so personal to himself and so intimate. I could never hope to imitate it. God and I have never understood one another."

"Why not? Couldn't you figure out who was who?"

"It is strange that you should mock me. I am trying to offer you your life."

"What makes you think saving me will keep God on your side?"

"My cause is just. To kill you would be unjust."

I shrugged. "Sounds good to me."

"It is so easy for you to make nothing of my cause. You came here into my country—the brash American who is knowing everything. But you cannot even begin to under-stand our struggle."

"I think I do understand your struggle, Governor," I said, sitting down on the bed, my heart still beating too fast. "You can't connect with God, but you need him to give you confidence. The thing is, he doesn't take kindly to his creatures negotiating with him for a share in the power. That's what you haven't understood yet."

Listen to me. I was in as bad a shape as poor Songo—a rebel lost, alone. What right did I have to lecture him? Stop it, I told myself. Kill the self-pity. There was a way out of this if only I could keep my big mouth under control.

"We will be holding you here," Saluso said, suddenly looking more relaxed. "After I take power, we will decide what must be done with you."

"My family?"

"I have no control over that, Ben. Perhaps you should pray."

"Isn't there any way you can call Murphy off them?"

"He's very angry. It will be great trouble to convince him to spare you, let alone your wife and children."

"Please."

"I will try."

He turned and walked out, the door locking behind him, a blighted little man trusting his Maker to support him because the cause seemed to be just. Who was more doomed—Songo or me?

CHAPTER ELEVEN

BEN

T he only hope I had left was to escape. For awhile I circled the cell, looking for weak spots, possible weapons, anything. I tried to take the bed apart, but everything that would normally be bolted was welded solid.

Saluso hadn't promised me my life, only a stay of execution. Now that Murphy had no further use for my family as hostages, he'd probably soon send orders to have them disappear forever. Why hadn't I done something to prevent this? Why hadn't I told Simpson to take a flying leap when he pressured me to take on a project clearly outside our parameters?

I'd been a fool all along the way—taking the family with me when I knew I was dealing with a possible revolutionary; believing that Saluso and Murphy were at odds with one another when they were still hand in hand; almost buying Saluso's story about being a misunderstood good guy.

But the worst was going along with Saluso's plot even when I knew there would probably be a coup at the end of it.

When I'd given in to Saluso, a cold wind had started churning in my chest, as if I'd been emptied of everything alive. Why should God stay in the heart of a man who'd only ever given lip service to his commitment to him?

A key rattled in the door, and it swung open. My watch showed just past nine.

"Mr. Sylvester?" It was Kdoma, the pilot. I'd taken a liking to him even though he worked for the wrong side. He smiled awkwardly at me.

"Are you my executioner?" I asked.

"No. I have brought you food." He signaled through the door, and a soldier carried in a tray—pounded yam, some kind of meat sauce over it, a banana, a Coke. Good food, hot and spicy, but it went into the cold void inside me and congealed there, making me feel as if I'd swallowed a pound of modeling clay. Kdoma said nothing, just watched me eat.

When I was done, I handed him back the tin plate and the fork and the Coke bottle. He made as if to speak, then shook his head and extended his arm in a handshake. Our palms touched, and I heard the crackle of paper. A tremor went through me, then he was gone and there was a note clutched in my fist.

As casually as I could, my heart beating faster, I lay down on the bed and turned to the wall, acting like a tired prisoner about to nap off his latest meal. The paper took me forever to open, my fingers clumsy and shaking. Then I could hardly read it in the limited light:

Mr. Sylvester,
Be prepared to leave quickly when I come for you. Do not question anything I should tell you to do, and do

not hesitate to obey me. This is your only opportunity, and your very life will depend on it.

No signature. For a few seconds more I stared at the note. Then I crumpled it and shoved it into my pocket, trying to figure out how to deal with the sudden ray of light when I'd already started preparing to die.

Option number one: This was a handy way for Murphy or Saluso to get rid of me. Either I'd be "shot while escaping" or Kdoma would leave my body somewhere in the jungle.

Option number two: Kdoma was on the level, acting as some kind of secret agent. I was being rescued and I'd find Karen and the kids and we'd all go back to our happy home in Lynden, Washington, and I'd promise never to have another adventure.

Right, and Kdoma was an angel sent by God because I was very sorry about doing the evil Saluso's bidding and God had decided to give me just one more chance. You have to understand that my whole life had been reduced to a tiny cell in a country where no one liked me. I was already a dead man, and now I had a note in my pocket that was either life or death, but I didn't know which.

I started wishing I could pray again. The old urge for transcendence comes back when you're squeezed into a corner too small for easy breathing. Losing God was like having a father die in your arms. But I wasn't about to cry out to him the moment I needed him even though I'd defied him when I had a chance to trust him. So I didn't try to pray.

When you're left with no option but death, something is

always worth more than nothing. I decided I'd go with Kdoma. If he shot me in the back as soon as we got into the jungle, it would be no worse than dying in a cell or on a parade ground.

Through the morning I began learning how to deal with being alone with nothing to do or read, no one to talk to. I've always had to be active, either accomplishing something or feeding my mind. Stripped of everything but my own thoughts, I began to suspect that I was approaching bankruptcy.

At least the cell was reasonably cool. Even though I was dripping, it was much hotter outside. Not that it mattered much. I probably wouldn't live long enough to appreciate the cooler weather to come.

Noon. Kdoma fed me again, this time saying nothing. Even when I made to speak, he shook his head, leaving as soon as I'd finished eating. The guy had my life in his hands, but his face was like a stone carving.

Ahead was the prospect of the afternoon stretching out, gray and ugly. Karen. Jack. Jimmie. The thought of them was an aching hole, painful beyond words, but I couldn't yet let any hope grow there. The possibility of having it dashed was too unbearable to think about.

I remembered a moment only a few weeks before when Jimmie had rushed into the house just before dinner, shouting that he'd found the biggest frog in the world, dragging me from my newspaper to see it. Sure enough, it had been a toad the size of a personal pizza, and all of us had spent the next half hour watching it hop across the lawn to safety. Jimmie's laughter hung in my memory.

Or Jack, the day he'd found a way to beat the video game he'd been fighting with for days, and the pride in his eyes when I recognized his amazing creativity.

While I lay on the bed, I dragged out the memories like a photo album, holding them out in front of me, reveling in them while I tried to stop Father Time from relentlessly beating out the minutes, cutting short whatever life I had before they came and shot me or freed me or locked me up forever or eliminated my family without a qualm.

Two o'clock, and with absolutely no warning, hell fell on the camp. An explosion, incredibly loud, close, debris falling heavily just outside the window. Then another, farther away, and another that blasted with awesome force no more than thirty feet from me. Shouting. Small arms fire hammering.

I ran to the window, seeing nothing but the alley, the noise incredible until the sound began fading as my ears gave up trying to function.

Then Kdoma was there, flinging open the cell door and shouting something at me, his voice silent because I couldn't hear anything anymore. He grabbed my arm and steered me out. Dazed, I let him drag me through the building. In front was a small green Peugeot, windows tinted black. He opened the door and pushed me into the passenger seat, taking the driver's seat for himself.

Lurching forward, we drove, feeling the concussion of nearby explosions, three jets streaking over us, low and deadly. Soldiers were everywhere, some of them bleeding from the ears, none of them seeming to have any idea where they were running.

Kdoma weaved the car through them, moving along the narrow paved roadway that led past the line of army barracks toward the airport. Most of the buildings were already on fire. Out on the parade ground we had to swerve to avoid fallen bodies—some dismembered—and fleeing soldiers. Craters kept bursting out on the tarmac as the jets dropped their horrors around us, the ground spewing dirt and asphalt all over the car.

We aimed for the gates at the end of the compound, still swerving, still alive, still hearing nothing but feeling every concussion. Then we were through, and the hell was behind us.

"What?" I said, not hearing my own voice. He couldn't hear me. "What's happening?" Useless. Both of us were deaf.

We'd emerged into a farming area about five miles from the nearest town. The terrain this far north was a mixture of bush and grassland, family agricultural plots dominating. But the road was crowded with people, most of them standing and staring at the blackening clouds rising over the base behind us, some of them running toward it like flies to a bug-light.

"Where are we going?" I asked, but Kdoma still couldn't hear me.

Gradually my ears began to ring and then faint sounds returned. We drove through a village, mainly mud and thatch houses but with some cement block homes with metal roofs. People were shouting excitedly to one another, pointing in the direction of the army base. No one was paying much attention to us.

Then we rounded a corner at the other end of town, right

into a roadblock, a large military truck sideways on the road, at least ten soldiers, all armed with automatic weapons.

"Who are they?" I shouted as we slowed to a stop.

"What?" he said. I could almost hear him, his voice a distant rumble.

"The soldiers. Do they work for Saluso?"

He flashed me a toothy smile, then rolled down the window no more than two inches and pushed a small wallet out of it. Within ten seconds, someone shoved the wallet back to him, and a soldier started the truck that had been blocking the road, moving it aside, giving us room. We pulled away from them free and clear.

Who was this guy? If these weren't Saluso's people, they had to be soldiers loyal to the federal government. Why had they let us go when we were obviously fleeing the army base their airborne buddies had just attacked? They must have known we'd come from Saluso.

"You're a federal agent," I shouted.

He touched one of his ears, shook his head and grinned.

"You've been a spy all along," I persisted. "Working for the national government. Saluso and Murphy never had a chance." My hearing was finally picking up, and I could dimly discern my own voice. Kdoma's must have been too.

"They had a chance, Mr. Sylvester. Everyone has a chance."

"Who are you?"

"Kdoma. I work for the president."

"A spy against Saluso?"

"Yes."

"So Saluso and Murphy never had a hope of bringing this off."

"They could have given up their foolish idea before the wrath of the law had fallen upon them."

"This is rich," I said.

We moved rapidly through more rural land, farm plots alternating with grass and clumps of jungle, the same red mud-thatch houses dotting the area.

"You're from the same tribe as Saluso, aren't you? He trusted you, but the whole thing was a bust before it even got off the ground. You guys knew all about the coup."

"The army base near the capital, the one you have not yet visited, is already secure," Kdoma said, dodging a large pothole. "We have taken full control of it this morning."

"The coup's over?"

"No. We do not yet have sufficient resources to be moving against the base you visited first. They possess ten jets, eight tanks, many men."

"So I'm in the middle of a civil war."

"In some manner of speaking."

"Am I going to be the prime defendant in a show trial when this is over?"

"Why?"

"I'm a traitor. I worked for Saluso."

"You did this only under much duress."

Another village, quieter than the last one. The army base was too far away now for the fighting to be heard. Kdoma pulled up at a "supermarket," equivalent in size to a 7-Eleven.

"Please remain in the car," he said, opening the door only

far enough to squeeze out and slam it again quickly. I wasn't crazy. The last thing I wanted was to be seen by someone.

After a few minutes, Kdoma came out with some bread and fruit, even a chunk of French cheese and the inevitable case of Coke. I was getting used to drinking warm pop. It was better than getting dysentery.

We moved on, covering the miles, tearing off chunks of bread and cheese and eating as we went. But we hadn't gone far before I couldn't hold back from asking my most important question. "My family…"

"Try not to worry. We are doing our best with that problem."

"We?"

"You and I."

"What's your plan exactly? Why did you rescue me from Saluso?"

"Are you sure you have actually been rescued?" He picked up an orange and bit into the skin. I took it and peeled it for him. "You have not given me an answer to my question," he said.

"It looked like a rescue to me. If you'd wanted to kill me, my body would be in the bush fifty miles back."

"I must explain some things to you, Mr. Sylvester." We approached a dirt side-road and Kdoma took it, our ride turning rough, deep puddles everywhere. "I am a police inspector working in our internal security department. I came into Governor Saluso's employment as a pilot a year ago, but he has been finding me useful for other things as well. Over the past year, he has grown to trust me with many confidences.

When your family went to Mr. Murphy's hotel, the governor insisted that I should go as well and make certain that Mr. Murphy brought no harm to your wife and your children."

"You've seen Karen?" I asked, blood rushing to my head.

"Yes, though I must tell you that the car your family was traveling in was fired on before they reached the hotel. It is in my understanding that the ones doing this deed were armed robbers, possibly dismissed soldiers. It is popular to rob the rich by killing them in their cars and then looting at will."

"Is my family safe?"

"The car had bullet-proofing. But Mr. Murphy thought the villains were agents of the federal government. That is why they hurried their planning for the coup. At first they had been intending to send you and your family out of the country a few weeks before the insurrection occurred so that the lies about the division between Mr. Murphy and the governor would have time to be believed as fact. After the events on the road to his hotel, with Mr. Murphy believing that federal soldiers had been sent to kill him—"

"They moved up the schedule for the coup," I finished. "What date did they set?"

"Next week," he said. "They had been expecting that your work would be complete and the generals would be believing that Mr. Murphy was no longer to be involved. Then the governor would order the generals to carry out the coup. But you have revealed the truth to these men and now I am having to save your life."

"Was it you who called in the jets back there?"

"Yes," he said. "They had strict orders not to attack your

prison or the car we are riding in."

"Karen and my boys—is there any way to rescue them now?"

Kdoma took his eyes of the road for a moment to give me a hard stare. "I am enduring considerable risks for you, Mr. Sylvester. My mission is over, and I am ordered to report to the president tomorrow. Instead, we are making this journey."

"Where to?"

"To the place where they were being hidden. The man who drove them to their new location has been influenced to reveal to us where they are. We must needs find them and remove all of you from this country."

CHAPTER TWELVE

KAREN

About four o'clock in the morning, Karen was suddenly startled awake by the sounds of gunfire, rapid shots from machine guns about a mile away or maybe even less. It woke the children too, it was that loud. For two or three minutes the firing went on, then there was only silence. By that time, the children were in bed with her, shivering. Both of them remembered the way they'd been shot at on their journey to Sid Murphy's hotel.

"Karen?" It was Tom's voice outside their door.

"Yes?" she said.

"Can you get yourself and the kids together and come out here?"

The boys were strangely silent as they dressed quickly and went out into the dining room to sit around the large table. Two kerosene lamps had been lit and hung from the ceiling because the power was out again. Tom and Kelly were dressed, and their faces showed deep concern, perhaps even some fear.

"It could have been just someone celebrating," Kelly said. "They do that sometimes."

But Tom disagreed with her. "There were too many shots for a celebration. They must have fired three hundred rounds."

"Your friend at the oil company warned you to leave the country," Karen said, hearing the fright in her voice, "and just before we went to bed, the night watchman told us there were soldiers in the jungle."

All of them deep down knew what it was, but none of them wanted to accept it yet, especially not at four in the morning. Karen had explained to them why Ben had come to Mtobe, and about his fears that Governor Saluso was intending to carry out a coup. Now it seemed the coup had started.

Why hadn't Tom and Kelly left the country as they'd been warned to do? Karen hated to think they'd stayed because she hadn't wanted to leave Ben, but their reasons were deeper than her fears for her husband. Tom and Kelly wouldn't leave until they were sure there was nothing else they could do but go. Even in these frightening hours before dawn, the sound of guns wasn't enough to make them flee.

They had a night watchman, a bright and enterprising man who always seemed to know everything that was happening in the area. Tom got up, went to the door, and called him. The man, who was about thirty-five, came in hesitantly. Even with egalitarian employers, Africa still had a class structure that was difficult for any African servant to overlook.

"Join us," Kelly said to him. "Coffee?"

He sat down uneasily, holding tight to the mug that was offered to him.

"What's happening out there?" Tom asked.

"There is trouble," he said softly. "I cannot understand it. Some of my friends are saying there is war."

"Who's fighting in this war?" Tom asked.

He shook his head and started to rise. "I am only a watchman."

"Please stay," Kelly said. "We have to understand this, and you've always been such a help to us."

He relaxed only a bit. "There is a large army encampment fifty miles to the north and west. They are saying that the soldiers there are become rebels. Armed men are moving toward the south."

"In this direction?" Tom's voice had an edge to it.

"Perhaps."

"What was that shooting?" Tom asked.

"I think the police. Or the soldiers in the jungle." By then the watchman was starting to look even more ill at ease.

"Those soldiers you told us about last night—are they from that rebel army camp?" Tom asked.

"I do not know who they are," he said. "Some people have been seeing them. Please, my work is done for this night. Am I permitted to go?"

"Could the rebels already have reached this area?" Tom asked.

"I do not know," he said.

The watchman went on his way, and they ate an uneasy early breakfast together. Something seemed very strange about the growing daylight, and Karen tried to think of what it might be. Then it came to her—there wasn't any noise.

Africans are boisterous and loud. They embrace life at full volume and drive their cars at incredible speed with horns blaring. But there were no voices calling to one another, and no cars passed, not even the taxis that someone at Sid's hotel had described to Karen as "flying coffins."

"We're not known as quitters," Tom said as they finished their meal. "A lot of people thought we were foolish to come here, but this is our home."

"Something terrible is happening, Tom," Kelly said.

"Are we supposed to run out on everyone just because we hear some shots and our night watchman says there are soldiers in the woods?" he asked.

"We've got Karen and the boys too," she said.

"No," Karen protested quickly, looking across at Jack and Jimmie. Jimmie was getting bored and was fidgeting with a fork. Jack seemed terribly frightened, his eyes filled with a haunted look that troubled her. "Please don't make your plans to accommodate us. I wish Sid Murphy hadn't pushed us on you."

"If he's been working on a coup and it's coming down now," Tom said, "he probably just wanted you distanced from him. It's not your fault."

"I don't want to influence your plans," Karen said.

"We haven't made any plans yet." Tom looked across the table at his wife. "What do you think?"

"Let's go to the U.S. consulate in _____ (she named a city) and find out what's happening."

Tom must have seen the anxiety on her face. "I'll get the van," he said.

Fleeing to the consulate seemed to all of them to be the wisest thing to do. If they left right away, perhaps they could outrun whatever armed forces were moving toward them.

They prayed together before they left the table, then Karen and the boys went to their bedroom and packed quickly. Kelly did the same while Tom filled the gas tank from reserve jerricans and added two more full ones to the luggage area of his van.

When they started out, Kelly stared back at her house. The look on her face told Karen that she feared it would be a long time before she came back, if she ever did.

Karen felt detached, as if watching herself and her children from a distance, unable to enter into this horrible world where people betrayed one another and war was never far away. The only one far away was God, who never should have allowed them to be in this situation.

"We better take the back road," Tom said, not sounding very certain about his choice. "They're less likely to block it than the main highway."

They drove out of town in the Volkswagen van and went down a narrow two-lane roughly paved road with small farms all along its edges. About two miles along, the first roadblock appeared—a long sawhorse across the road and four or five African men wearing dark blue. They slowed down and stopped.

"Your driving license, please," said the person who appeared to be in charge. Tom handed the man his license.

"Who are they?" Karen whispered to Kelly.

"Police," she said. "Roadblocks are a regular feature

around here because of the armed robberies lately."

"Where is your destination?" their leader asked. He was a big man with a high-pitched voice.

"The nearest U.S. consulate," Tom answered. "We heard there's trouble."

"You must be going back at once. The road ahead is too dangerous."

"What's happening?" Tom asked. "Can you tell us anything?"

The policeman looked surprised. Karen supposed civilians in Mtobe didn't normally ask the police for information.

"You will be safe at home," he said firmly. "Go back."

"How can you be sure of that?" Tom asked.

Kelly touched his arm. "Don't push him, Tom."

"We're going on," Tom said. "Either arrest us or open the barricade."

"I have been ordered to let no one pass," the policeman said.

"Why? What's ahead?"

"Tom!" Kelly said, now looking frightened.

But the policeman was becoming confused. "There are gatherings of rebel soldiers," he finally admitted. "An army encampment north of here has become insane. Even two of our men have been killed this morning."

"That's why we want to get to the consulate," Tom said. "The danger is right here, all around us. We need to go where it's safer."

"If you die on the way, I will be blamed," the policeman told him.

"Maybe we should go back, Tom," Kelly said. "Our African friends will stand with us."

"Craig warned us to get out," Tom said, "and I should have listened." He turned back to the policeman. "We want to go on. Here"—he reached into a compartment and pulled out a pen and a piece of paper—"I'll write a letter accepting full responsibility for whatever happens. No one will blame you."

Along the road several miles outside the town, they came upon a side lane with a sign pointing to a Bible college. Tom turned his van into this lane as if he had driven to this place many times before.

"Do we have to, Tom?" Kelly asked, her voice full of nervous tension.

"They might know something. Besides, somebody has to be told where we've gone."

The Bible college occupied a large campus with a soccer field in the middle and several homes around the edges. Across the field was the main college building, low and long and painted in a two-tone green. Students were playing a game of soccer on the field.

An older African man came out of his house, and when Tom saw him, he stopped the van and walked over to the man. They talked for about fifteen minutes, then Tom came back looking troubled.

"Well?" Kelly said as they turned onto the main road again.

"Nothing," he said. "We've got forty miles to go, so let's just get there."

"Tell me, Tom," Kelly said sharply.

"Federal soldiers have been seen in the area for a week. The radio says an attempted coup has been put down with minimal loss of—"

"A coup? Where?" Karen shouted her words, startling everyone.

Tom hesitated, then said, "Governor Saluso's state."

"That's where Ben is," she said. "He's with Saluso."

"I know."

"Who are the soldiers in the area?" Kelly broke in. "Are they part of this coup?"

Tom didn't respond. None of them had an answer. The horror of the situation was too much for anyone, even someone who belonged to God and trusted in him. The cry of Karen's heart was simple—Why are you doing this?—but he didn't answer her. She felt tears rising in her eyes, not just because she was afraid but because she was shocked at the intensity of her anger. Unbidden, the accusation came into her mind: I thought you loved us.

They decided to go on down the road leading to the consulate. If the soldiers they'd heard about were rebels, they'd probably been sent ahead to take control when the coup actually started. But since the country was quite large, any rebel soldiers would be spread thin. At least that's the way Tom explained it to them while they drove. There wouldn't be enough of a rebel army to do much harm in any one location, but there would be enough of them to endanger the lives of a carload of civilians.

Ten more miles went by, and still they saw no signs of trouble. They started breathing easier as they passed farm after farm. They didn't see any cars, only the usual large number of people walking and cycling. Karen had been in Africa long enough by that time to know that something must be wrong if no taxis were operating. What was more, everyone stared at them as they passed. Some people pointed, and some even shouted, though she couldn't understand what they were saying.

And then suddenly the danger they feared became a reality. On the road ahead, about twenty men dressed in green army uniforms stood side by side, each one holding a large weapon. They looked like a firing squad, and Karen realized with a deep sense of dismay that they'd risked and lost.

"Don't let them know you're Ben's wife," Tom said. His voice was unnaturally calm given the circumstances. The soldiers, all twenty of them, formed a half-circle around them, each soldier pointing his gun at them.

"Mommy?" Jimmie squealed, climbing up on Karen's lap and clinging to her. Jack put his arm around her and shut his eyes. His teeth were clenched.

She felt certain the soldiers planned to shoot them. She waited for the shots to come and prayed that Ben at least would survive. I don't blame you, Ben, she thought. You couldn't have known, not like God knows.

They sat in the van in complete silence and stared at the dark holes in the ends of the guns and waited to die. Time was frozen. Why didn't they shoot? Why didn't they just get it over with?

Then someone shouted a brusque order and each soldier took a step back. Three of them pulled the doors of the van open.

"Get out," a soldier shouted. They did what they were told. "Lie on the ground, face down. There." The pavement was wet from the rain that had fallen a few minutes before, but none of them thought to argue with him.

Karen found herself praying the same words over and over—"Spare my children, spare my children, spare my children." Why didn't they shoot? They lay together on the cold road and waited.

Karen wished she could have held Ben one more time.

CHAPTER THIRTEEN

BEN

The clock ticked in the living room of the small house we were staying in as I slipped in and out of sleep, the chair hard against my back. I endured it because I needed the rest, but I envied our hosts their beds.

The first day after the initial excitement had been frantic. Kdoma had driven us deep into the bush, taking dirt tracks and trying to head southeast. There wasn't any need for maps because this was his home territory, and he never missed a beat. Neither did the car, for which I was grateful. I'd heard that Peugeots tend to die in water over a foot deep.

Once I started coming down from the shock of being rescued and then navigating a war zone, my big questions were about Kdoma. As a federal police inspector, what power did he have? What obstacles would we face while he tried to get us to Karen?

So I asked, and he told me the bad news. While the army base nearest the national capital was fully neutralized, and the one we'd just left was in chaos, the third base northeast of us was still in the game. Worse than the fact that they had ten jet fighters and several tanks, they had sent about a thousand men, in squads of twenty, into the countryside to take control of local governments and police when the coup began. These squads were everywhere. Kdoma wasn't sure what kinds of communications they had with home base, if any.

We stopped mid-afternoon, deep in the bush, at a place owned by Kdoma's brother's cousin or some such relation. A husband, wife, five kids all in a four-room house plus a detached kitchen in the back. They didn't have any extra beds, so Kdoma and I insisted on sleeping on chairs in the living room.

The tick of the clock was hypnotizing, but I wasn't finding it easy to sleep upright. The chair was too hard, and my brain wouldn't stop firing on all cylinders.

Strange dreams were part of the baggage I'd carried since God and I parted company. It was as if my evil twin took over every time I drifted into sleep. I never could remember any details, only smoke and chaos and people shouting at me in anger, murder on their minds. Dreams like that had been part of the reason I'd turned to God in the first place.

I woke near dawn with vague stirring sounds beginning outside. Someone went by on a motorcycle, bicycles squeaked along the bumpy track in front of the house, a servant girl began sweeping the dirt outside to decimate the bug population in the yard.

A couple of little boys ran into the room and stopped, their eyes wide with shock until they remembered we'd been staying overnight. When I nudged Kdoma in the other chair, he slid into wakefulness with amazing speed, instantly alert and ready for the day.

The rest of the kids bounded into the room noisily and made us the center of their attention until the novelty wore off. After a trip out back to clean up and try to shave, we shared breakfast with the family. They didn't seem to think it strange to have extra people at their table, the African spirit of hospitality fully at work.

"We must go," Kdoma said as soon as we were done, leading me out with only a brief "Thank you" to our hosts. Dawn was moving in fast. In the tropics, night turns to day in twenty minutes.

"How far now?" I asked as we got into the car.

"If we have no trouble, we should arrive this afternoon."

"You know where they are?" I asked.

"I know where they have been some days ago, but with rebel troops being everywhere, our journey and their location are too far from certain."

"If we do find them, what do you plan to do?"

"To remove all of you from the country. Your involvement with the governor has made you unwelcome."

"Do you have a way to get us across the border?"

"It is better if you do not know."

"Come on, Kdoma."

"It is a secret." From the tone of his voice, nothing short of torture would make him reveal it.

The bush road got worse every minute we drove. Where there wasn't deep water, erosion had taken away huge chunks of dirt, making me grateful that the Peugeot had a narrow wheelbase. A couple of times we dipped alarmingly, and once we got totally bogged. Since Kdoma wasn't letting me be seen outside, he had to push while I took the wheel and drove us out of the hole.

We avoided all but the smallest villages, giving me a view of Africa not many westerners see. I tried hard to pay attention to the scenery, anything to divert my attention from the horrifying realities: I was on the run both from federal authorities and rebel soldiers, in a place where anarchy had been pre-programmed. I still wasn't sure I trusted Kdoma. I wouldn't believe Karen and the kids were safe until I saw the whites of their eyes.

Midmorning. The terrain was more hilly now, the jungle dense except where farms had been hacked out of it. We were making good time over the rough road, Kdoma driving far faster than he should have with the visibility limited by corners, hills, and valleys.

We rounded a curve, doing about forty, and suddenly they were just ahead of us, maybe two hundred yards, an army squad camped on both sides of the road, soldiers packing up tents, jeeps in a row to one side.

Kdoma gunned it, slewing wildly as the tires tried to grab the sandy soil roadbed. We rocketed toward them, doing sixty, hoping for the best. But I could see a couple of soldiers, who had been lying down in the shade of one of the jeeps, rolling, pointing their rifles, firing.

Kdoma weaved like a stock car driver as something clanged into the Peugeot on his side. He shuddered beside me as we almost slid into a palm tree, and then we were past, shots still coming at us but out of range. No one followed us as we climbed a hill and turned a corner out of sight of them.

"Some driving!" I shouted, looking at Kdoma. "They missed—" I stopped. Kdoma was biting his lower lip, his face tensed up. "You all right?" I asked.

He didn't answer, just drove another mile then pulled over in a small clearing. The nearest house was a couple of hundred yards away.

"Kdoma," I said.

"A glancing blow only. Help me stop the bleeding."

I leaned across him. The door on his side was broken in, and his left pant leg was oozing blood across the top of it. The bullet must have kept going. I looked behind me and there was a hole in the corner window on my side, just past where the outer edge of my chest had been.

"How's the pain?" I asked.

"Bearable. We must stop the bleeding. There is a box in there." He motioned to the glove compartment.

We got his pants down. It was a graze, but fairly deep, blood oozing everywhere, the gouge at least half an inch deep and three inches long. He'd sport a dandy scar for the rest of his life. Patching it took only five minutes, and Kdoma was grateful for the antibiotic cream and bottle of Tylenol. He didn't hesitate to gulp a couple down, and one more for good measure.

"Can you drive?" I asked.

"One has no need of a left leg to pilot an automatic transmission car. The pain can be tolerated."

"How far do we need to go today?"

"About seventy miles. My uncle's cousin has a home there. Your wife's location was about forty miles farther, but we cannot reach it today." He grimaced, his teeth clenched.

"I'll drive."

"This is Africa," he said. "I can maintain a better speed."

"Maybe the soldiers who shot you have radioed ahead."

"I doubt they have radio communications. The only telephones in this area are at the post offices, and those are guarded by the police."

"Why are these rebel squads still skulking around in the bush?"

"The coup was to come in two days from now." Kdoma started driving. "Most people in Africa have short-wave receivers. I believe these soldiers have been sent as advance forces. When the radio stations began broadcasting news of the coup, they were to take control of local police and politicians. Instead, they are hearing that the coup is defeated and they are abandoned."

"That means they've got nothing to lose," I said. "Whether they surrender or fight it out, the best they can hope for is prison. The worst is death."

"They are desperate men." Kdoma winced as he bounced us through a pothole.

"Why didn't you tell me what we were facing?"

"What good would it have been doing?"

"Karen and the kids are in even more danger than I thought. I..." My voice trailed off as an overwhelming sense of déjà vu began to smother me. This was how it had been a year before when Karen disappeared and I bulled into it with the old Ben Sylvester bravado. People died, one of them a very good person. I swore to myself that it would never—

"Why is it, Ben," Kdoma said, "that so much of you is

hidden? You seem to be carrying a great darkness inside you."
Uncharacteristic words for an African.

"It's my life. Leave it alone."

"You have a faith…or you had one. Something has happened to you. If we are going to face trouble together, I must understand the pain in your soul." He steered around a turn and the car slid sideways. I grabbed an armrest as he hit the gas and sped on.

"Why did they shoot at us?" I asked, ignoring his questions.

"This car. It bears no markings but its manufacture and the tinted windows are usually to be found only on an official vehicle."

"That means every squad we meet will fire on the car."

"It is probable." His words were slurred slightly and I noticed he was suddenly driving very fast, taking chances I never would have. Too fast. We were going too fast.

"Kdoma!"

"What?" he said. "Let me drive." His voice was thick, words fuzzy at the edges. We barely made the corner, Kdoma oversteering. Then we hit a pothole hard and bottomed out.

"Stop. You'll kill us," I shouted. A goat sped by, missed by inches. "Stop!" I reached over and shut off the ignition and we coasted to a stop.

He stared at me. I expected a question, but it didn't come. Maybe it was the dark color of his pants that had kept me from noticing how much he was bleeding. But now, with the reckless driving, I looked at the car seat. It was soaked red.

"You're losing blood," I said. "A lot of it. We have to get help."

He didn't protest when I took over the driving and demoted him to navigator. It was terrifying to see him bleeding, maybe bleeding to death while I drove, weaving down the narrow road. People continued to throng everywhere, on most every form of transportation. But there were few cars, not even taxis. Were we too deep into the jungle for them to venture there?

"We need a doctor," I reminded Kdoma after another half hour of driving.

"Twenty minutes," he said, his diction fuzzier still. "There is a leprosy hospital."

"A what?"

"A British doctor works there. A beautiful place." His face was covered with sweat despite the air conditioning. "I am very cold. Thirsty." I shut the air conditioning off.

"You're bleeding badly. We don't have much time."

"Stay on this road for five miles. Then turn right at the petrol stand." He reclined the seat back and shut his eyes while I put on more speed. The dirt road was less crowded in this area, and I took every advantage I could.

There was no sign of more soldiers, and the few people out at midday were going about their usual business. But that didn't mean we wouldn't come upon a bunch of soldiers around the next corner.

I took a right at the gas station (one pump, hand-controlled, no sign) and followed a narrowing track that opened onto a large grassy compound, a few houses at one end and a hospital complex at the other. Between them was an abundance of flowering trees and a church building that probably seated two hundred. Kdoma was right—it was beautiful.

"Is it safe?" I asked.

"We will be safe here. We must be. There is nowhere else."

"Wouldn't a place like this be an easy target to take hostages?" We drove toward the houses, both of us scanning the landscape with our eyes.

"The soldiers are afraid of lepers. They will stay away from this place." He didn't sound like he'd convinced himself fully.

"You're not afraid of people with leprosy?"

"This is not the time for being afraid." His voice was very faint. "Take me to the doctor quickly. That house there."

I hoped he knew what he was doing. If I lost Kdoma, I might as well put a bullet in my head before either the federal soldiers or Saluso's men got me. Only Kdoma knew where Karen and the kids were.

I felt desperately alone.

CHAPTER FOURTEEN

KAREN

The sergeant in charge of the soldiers who had captured them was becoming dangerous. His rages were wilder and more frightening by the hour. He burst into the house regularly to yell at them until he got tired, then he'd turn and leave them just as abruptly as he had entered.

The complaint he kept making was that the governor's coup would have succeeded if the American CIA hadn't sent spies into Mtobe. His captives were American, and whether or not he ever believed they were spies, they represented to him the system that had destroyed his career, perhaps even his very life. He told them he had his men to care for and now none of them had any hope left.

The soldiers hadn't shot them after all while they lay on the wet road. They'd only searched the five of them roughly and then forced them into a small cement house nearby. Now Tom and Kelly, Karen and her children were cramped into a place no bigger than Karen's largest bedroom in Lynden. Someone had reinforced the windows and ceiling with pieces of aluminum, and the heat inside was almost unbearable.

Karen could well understand why these rebel soldiers were so afraid. The coup was over before it had even had a chance to begin. They had been left alone in enemy territory, and the best they could hope for was to be executed quickly when the federal army came searching for them.

The captives had mats on the floor for beds, a couple of stools to take turns sitting on, and a smelly bucket in the corner which a soldier came and emptied every few hours. But they also had prayer, which they uttered endlessly.

Tom got an idea on the second day. At first, it sounded foolish to them, but they didn't have any other solutions to offer, and so they started to pay more attention to it as the day went on. It depended on having the sergeant calm down enough to listen, but the afternoon of the second day went by and he was still wild with fear and anger, ranting at them every few hours.

The children had nothing to entertain themselves with, and they were starting to raise a fuss, especially Jimmie, who had never been one to enjoy being cooped up. Karen, Kelly, and Tom told them stories, sang to them, and helped them act out Bible stories and fairy tales. But just when they were playing happily, the sergeant would come in and scream at everyone.

"They won't hurt us," Tom told the boys once just after the sergeant left. "We're hostages. That means they want to keep us safe."

But the plan he'd come up with seemed so weak to Karen that she felt a pain in her chest just thinking about it. If the sergeant accepted Tom's idea, they could be facing even more danger than they were already in.

Late evening on the second day, the sergeant came in again, looking subdued and exhausted. Their prayers that he would calm himself enough to listen to them must have been working. He sat down heavily on a stool and stared for a few moments at Tom.

"Do you know why we are here together?" he asked.

"You were sent out to control this territory after the coup." Tom's voice was soft. "But the coup is over and you've lost. I suppose the loyal soldiers will have captured you before the week is out."

"We will make you to be shields for us," the sergeant said. "No one will shoot if we have you with us."

"But you can't keep us here as shields forever," Tom told him.

"There are other countries. We can take you with us until we are safe."

"Other countries that will welcome rebel soldiers?" Tom asked. "I don't think so."

"We would not be having this predicament if you CIA stayed at home where you belong."

Tom began pressing the sergeant, and Karen started to pray with all her heart. Even the kids were still, perhaps sensing that something significant was about to happen.

"Sergeant, you can make us hostages and get to the border, maybe even across it, but no other country wants to take in failed revolutionaries." The sergeant remained silent, and Tom went on. "Do you have a family?"

"Yes," he said.

"Children?"

"Yes."

"You'll lose everything once you cross the border."

The sergeant leaned back abruptly on his stool and almost tipped it over. "Do not be taking me for a fool," he said. "I was educated in mission schools, and I am much aware of the power of westerners to use their crafty words to weave a spell over the gullible African."

"I'm talking about your survival—you and your men. Listen to me and then decide. Okay?"

He didn't respond to Tom, only gave him a sideways glance. Tom pressed on.

"Your problem is that you're on the losing side. You're isolated in alien territory, and all you have to bargain with is us."

"I am well aware of my problem," the sergeant said.

"What if you had a way to ingratiate yourself with the army—the loyal army?"

"How?"

"Instead of being a kidnapper, why not become a rescuer?"

"I—" The sergeant realized what Tom was saying, and the trace of a smile came into his face. "What if," he said, "what if we found you on a dangerous road? I and my men never supported the coup. We were forced to obey orders. When we found you..."

"When you found us," Tom said, "we were very frightened. There were rumors of hostile rebel soldiers everywhere. All we wanted was to get to the nearest U.S. consulate."

"And so we decided to provide a guard for you," the sergeant said, a genuine smile now on his lips. "It was the best thing we could be doing because you were in danger, and we never supported the coup at all."

Tom held up his hand. "This isn't a fairy story, sergeant. Chances are the loyal soldiers will shoot you anyway."

"Tom!" Kelly said.

"I'm not going to lie to him," Tom said. "Look, sergeant, we want to live, and this is a better way of doing it than acting as your shields while you try to shoot your way across the border. I know you have to do what's best for you and your men. That probably isn't trying to leave the country, but I can't guarantee that even leading us into safe hands will win you any points with the government."

"And we may have to be fighting with other rebels like ourselves," the sergeant said. "Any of them that see you may want to capture you as hostages for themselves."

"We'll face that when we have to," Tom told him. Hope had begun to glow on Tom's face. All of them knew the risks involved.

There was planning to be done. They couldn't travel at night because the rebel soldiers in the countryside would set up roadblocks everywhere to stop the police or other enemies from moving around in the darkness. The soldiers who had captured them had hidden three trucks in the jungle behind the house where they'd been held captive. They would have to leave Tom's van behind.

While the sergeant went to tell his men about this new opportunity for survival, the captives had a chance to discuss what had happened. Tom's plan was not really an easy solution for them, and he wanted them to look at all the possible outcomes.

They'd be riding in the back of a stuffy truck out of the sight of curious eyes. With rebel troops everywhere—all of them desperate for some sort of way out—they could expect serious trouble along the way. They couldn't even trust the sergeant himself not to turn against them if it suited his purposes. Besides all those fears, they knew the loyal troops were on their way.

As best she could, Karen explained the situation to the boys. Jimmie was frightened. He didn't want anything more to do with men with guns. But Jack's reaction was strange, even for him. He didn't seem to be frightened any longer. His emotion was more like anger, his eyes accusing Karen of what? Of being an incompetent parent? Of abusing him? Of being the one who was supposed to protect him but couldn't?

She found it disturbing even though she had no time or energy to deal with it then. Jack was changing, and it frightened her to see the anger boiling inside of him. Too many terrible things had happened to a boy as sensitive as Jack. He still had his soft moments when he'd let her stroke his hair, but whenever something reminded him of their troubles, the anger was close to the surface.

Morning arrived and rain was falling. After they'd pushed Tom's van deeper into the jungle, they got into the back of what was to be the third truck in their convoy, riding along with three soldiers who started joking with each other the moment they began moving down the road. Three army trucks in broad daylight would be anything but subtle or secretive, but there really was no other choice. The only chance they had was to take the many dirt roads that criss-crossed the countryside, travel by day, and hope that the jungle would shelter them until they reached the consulate and the sergeant delivered them into safe hands.

But it seemed like such a gamble to Karen. Choose this road and hope those who would harm them had chosen another one. She feared it would be only a matter of time before they came into a confrontation.

The cloth flap over the back of the truck was down to hide their white faces. It was very hot. By midmorning Karen felt limp. Jack was silent except when he was asking for some of the food or water the sergeant had provided for them. Jimmie fidgeted and talked constantly.

The narrow dirt roads were in poor condition, and every jolt was painful.

"How far is it?" Karen asked after half an hour.

"I'd guess maybe fifty miles or so," Tom said, "considering the twists and turns we're taking."

Fifty miles on an American freeway was less than an hour. Here it could take them all day long.

Then suddenly their truck swerved violently and stopped. There were loud voices and the sounds of other vehicles start-ing their engines. They waited anxiously, unable to show themselves, frightened and praying. Finally the voices died away and several trucks went by.

When the sergeant opened the flap to talk to them, his face showed considerable strain. He climbed inside and sat on the bench after motioning for the soldiers to get out of the truck.

"You people are poison in my bones," he said. "It would have been better to leave you in the jungle."

"We're your only hope," Tom told him flatly. "I thought you understood that."

"I'm not a fool!" There was intense anger in the sergeant's voice. Karen was relieved that she couldn't see his face very well in the darkness.

"What happened?" Tom asked him.

"We have come upon another group of our soldiers. They are as frightened as we are, but we have not told them about you."

"Do they have any news?"

"Yes." They waited while he paused for effect. "You are prisoners. Why should I inform you?"

"We're not prisoners. You are rescuers." Tom was pressing hard, and Karen hoped he knew what he was doing.

"The federal air force has been mobilized. They have orders to destroy all of us unless we surrender," the sergeant said.

"How do you know that?" Kelly asked.

"It's on the news on the radio."

"So surrender," Tom said.

"You have told me that we will be safe, but there is too much fear in all of us. We cannot find a way to communicate with the president's forces to tell them that we have rescued you."

"Can the air force see our trucks?" Karen heard herself asking.

"Of course. They will no doubt be destroying us sometime today."

"Do you have a faith?" Tom asked, his voice gentle.

"I was raised in a mission school, but that was a long time ago." The sergeant got up abruptly, and as he jumped down off the truck, he turned and said, "Pray for us."

As soon as he was gone, Jack asked, "What have the jets got—bombs or bullets or what?"

"We're not going to see any jets," Karen said.

"Don't lie to me!" he shouted, starting to cry.

"I don't know," she said. "You heard the sergeant. I don't know if he's right. None of us do."

"You're supposed to take care of us. Jimmie and me."

Karen wanted to cry. "This is the way life can be sometimes, Jack. I'm sorry you had to grow up so soon, and I'm very sorry we came here. I'm sorry…" With nothing more to say, she was glad when the soldiers came back in and the truck started moving again.

Years before, Ben and Karen had seen *Das Boot,* the German film about life on a U-boat during the Second World War. Now Karen regretted having seen it. She felt the same fear as she rode in that truck, like huddling in a tin can, waiting for a big bully to drop a rock on top of it. Ben was still on her mind, but the terror of the moment sapped most of her attention.

An hour passed. They hung onto the benches they were sitting on and prayed. The hardest part was not being able to see anything, only to hear the engine, puddles splashing under them, every bump and hole in the road causing rattles and creaks.

Then suddenly jets came streaking in over their heads, the

noise appallingly loud, and powerful explosions went off right next to them. Their truck swerved off the road into the bush or into some farmer's field. Karen grabbed the children and dragged them to the floor even before the truck stopped bouncing. Something nearby blew up with a roar beyond imagining. Bullets started hitting their truck, flying everywhere and bouncing off the metal, while the roar of the jets drowned out their thoughts.

How long was it before the jets stopped passing over and they were left in silence, the only sounds the crackling of fire outside and Jimmie crying?

They were alive, but Karen felt nothing inside her but fear and anger. She'd lived for God with all of her heart, had even led her husband to him. Now her husband was lost without even a kiss good-bye. Her children were sprawled under her, listening to the countryside burn. Whether they survived or not, she knew her anger would stay until God told her why he hadn't put a stop to everything before it got this far.

The sergeant opened the flap finally, his face covered with soot and tears. When they saw him, the three soldiers in the back didn't need to hear any order from him to get out. They went with speed, leaving the captives alone with the weeping sergeant.

"What's happened?" Tom asked.

"We are destroyed," the sergeant answered him, angrily brushing aside his tears. "The other two trucks are destroyed. Every man is dead. There are just now the four of us left and you white people."

"I'm sorry," Tom said.

"Yes, the other trucks are destroyed," he said. "This one has a broken rear axle. We are finished."

CHAPTER FIFTEEN

BEN

The angels were singing, reaching a crescendo, the word *glory* forming a rolling rhythm that seemed to have no end. I shut my eyes so the sound of it could seep into my soul, there in the little mud church in the middle of the bush.

This was a choir like none I'd ever seen or heard of—sporting missing fingers, feet with no toes, faces marked and scarred. Leprosy patients. Their joy was as unmistakable as it was baffling.

It was Sunday, the day after we'd driven onto the ground of the leprosy hospital with Kdoma in bad shape, almost incoherent. Doctor Evelyn Carlson—a woman from England who'd been in Africa forever—took two minutes to find the second bullet hole in Kdoma's leg, the one that explained the amount of blood everywhere when we eased him out of the passenger seat. So much for my career in diagnosis. She got the slug out fairly easily since the car door had slowed the velocity.

But there weren't any supplies for a transfusion. Kdoma

would have to rebuild on his own, and it would be at least a week before he could even ride in a car. One week at least, stuck in a leprosy compound. Even then, Kdoma probably couldn't drive. And with rebel soldiers in the woods, our travel options were nil. That's why I was sitting in this little church and listening to the lepers' choir, every one of them more joyful than any leper should be.

By the bottom of the week, we'd probably have the whole rebel army ringed around us, and I was sure they'd love a nice white hostage like me. Karen and the boys—Ben Sylvester couldn't help them, couldn't help himself. I couldn't even pray.

At the front of the church was a flower centerpiece at least four feet across, made with multi-colored blooms picked in the jungle, a visual counterpart to the amazing music. I sat there drinking it in, trying to find some measure of healing for the pain.

Finally the singing stopped and the pastor started his sermon. He wasn't speaking English.

"He's telling the story of the thieves on the cross." It was the doctor suddenly beside me, whispering. I hadn't seen her come in. "One of them died cursing. The other found peace and hope."

My first urge was to tell her not to bother translating, but she was pushing sixty-five and she'd given most of those years to Africa, to God. Her devotion was her reason for being. I didn't have the heart to tell her she had no understanding of the losses I'd suffered—my family, a God I'd only just begun to know.

"The pastor is asking, 'Which thief is you? Will you go to

your grave arguing with the Christ? Or will you find your peace today?'"

I wanted to tell her to stop; it was too hard to listen to words like that. Instead, I let her preach the whole sermon, phrase by phrase. Maybe I got tired from the effort it took to stay numb to what I was hearing, but strangely, while I sat there in a church full of lepers, listening to a preacher I couldn't understand except through an interpreter, my battered mind, unbidden, started telling me the truth.

Ben Sylvester, it said, is coward extraordinaire, too terrified to trust God when it counted, when it mattered. Saluso would have let you go, but you thought the risk was too great. Look at these people. Lepers, castoffs, abandoned by family and friends. The doctor has told you that even some of the nurses are afraid to touch them. And there they are singing. What does that tell you, Ben? What does that say to you?

If you knew there was at least a chance that Saluso would have sent you home safely even though you'd told him to take a flying leap—if you understood that helping him gave you no guarantees—

Where's the real courage, Ben? Is it in taking your life in your hands, riding the wave, fighting the unbeatable foe? The thief on the cross could have fought and cursed his way to the grave, but where would it have gotten him? Where has it gotten you?

Better to trust the god you can see than the God you can't, is that your credo now? Never give God an even break until he drops you into a leprosy hospital and makes you listen to people who really have no reason to hope?

The sermon ended and the choir got up to sing one more time. You have to understand that I'd run out of resources. When the choir started singing—those lepers who had no reason to praise anyone let alone God—I saw how useless it was to think that I could ever muscle him away again. No matter how much you fight or how smart you are, you always come to the end of yourself one day.

And so (wearily, mind you) I said, "Yes." Nothing more. And I'd swear he sat down next to me, displacing the doctor who hadn't heard what I said to him. God, sitting next to me, invisible, awesomely powerful, telling me, "There isn't any need to be afraid."

"I can't fight any more," I said.

"It's already forgiven," he said.

I had no illusions that he'd transformed me into an instant saint. "Don't you realize," I said to him—God, sitting beside me—"don't you understand how unreliable I am, how easy it is to wander away from you and do something stupid? Why should you forgive me? What have I done to deserve your help now?"

Me lecturing God. What a picture that must have been in the courts of heaven. I listened to the choir, exuberant, and I shared with them the fierce joy, born of the painful recognition that God is God, and you either face life with him, no matter what, or you shrivel up and expire in lonely self-reliance.

"Do you think I abandon my people as easily as that?" he asked. "Do you really believe you have so little value to me?"

"I failed the test."

"What makes you think it was a test? Could it not have been a genuine offer of help?"

"I knew Saluso would have released me. He made sure he didn't tell me anything."

"And you made the wrong choice?"

"Of course I made the wrong choice."

"I wanted to hear you say it."

I knew then what he was telling me: It was over. It was time to end this. All he'd wanted from me was my repentance and trust. That's all he'd ever wanted.

A final burst of praise ended the service, and I sat there watching everyone file out until only the doctor and I were left. With an awkward smile, she motioned to me that it was time to go. We walked back to her house in silence.

When we got there, Kdoma was awake. He looked awful, and I was quickly ordered out of his bedroom while Dr. Carlson changed his dressings. It was hard not to keep reminding myself that this guy was my lifeline, and he couldn't be hurt as badly as he was—not if I ever wanted to see Karen and the boys again. But I would. I knew that now.

Eventually the doctor came out and told me Kdoma wanted to talk to me. From the look on her face, she obviously thought it was a bad idea. "Fifteen minutes," she said. "Not one second more."

I went in and found him looking a bit more comfortable except for the lines of strain on his face. "Ben," he said. "I must speak with you. I have been lying here with just a nurse to watch over me, and God says that I must tell you."

"Tell me what? Rest, Kdoma. There's time for talking later."

"I have to tell you now." He grimaced as a wave of pain struck him. Then he started to talk, and what he had to tell me was enough to shake me back down the same dark hole I'd fallen into before the lepers sang. Hang on.

"For more than a year," he said, "I have been in the governor's employment. He trusted me and he has been too careless about revealing information."

"That's because he thinks he's God," I murmured.

"We have known, Ben—we have known of the plannings for the coup for many months."

"Why didn't you try to stop it?"

"The oil companies could not be stopped so easily as the governor might be. If we arrested the governor or the generals who have been plotting with him, Mr. Murphy would find someone else to lead a coup. We needed to bring discredit to all of them, even Mr. Murphy and the oil companies."

"Why do I need to know this now?" I asked. "Get some rest first." I got up to leave.

"Stay," he said. "Please stay. There is more." He paused, fighting pain and exhaustion. "We knew of you, Ben, long before you came here. We discovered everything of the governor's plan to force you to pretend to be an official of the American government."

"And you didn't try to head us off? What's wrong with you people? I brought my family here—my wife and two little kids—and you knew in advance what Saluso and Murphy were going to do to us?"

"My superiors insisted that you were necessary. I believe they were hoping to seize your false documents as soon as you had convinced the generals of their authenticity. Then the government would pretend that the documents were genuine and would be using them to discredit the oil companies."

"Wouldn't the State Department shout long and hard that they were forgeries?"

"What good would it be doing?" Kdoma asked. "We would simply say that it is normal for a foreign government to deny that it interfered with the internal affairs of another country."

"But I destroyed the documents."

"That was the second blow against us. The first was the attack on Mr. Murphy's car when it was transporting your family to his hotel. Mr. Murphy had the belief that the assailants were agents of the federal government who suspected that he was plotting something and wanted to remove him."

"So he and Songo moved up the date for the coup, and you didn't have everything in place yet to stop them."

"That is correct. We forced the encampment near the national capital to surrender, and we bombed the encampment you were in—at great risk to both of us—but it was far more important to stop the insurrection than to spare our lives. However, the final general of the three—the first one you had visited—has acted too quickly, and we are not yet controlling him."

"So it got out of hand, and now my wife and kids are in rebel held territory," I said.

"Can you forgive me?" Kdoma whispered, his voice very weak now.

"You were only doing what you had to," I said.

"Do not say such a thing, Ben. I have been resisting this plan of my superiors for some time now, especially when I learned that you were bringing your wife and children. How are we to take our place as an important nation if we sacrifice innocent people to carry out our purposes?"

"Don't talk," I said. His face was gray with exhaustion. But I was amazed at my own reaction. The Ben Sylvester I knew would have been churning with fury. Instead, I felt like mush. I couldn't condemn Kdoma when I'd so recently been given such a keen and disturbing vision of myself.

After a simple lunch, I went and sat in the living room. Kdoma had faltered through a few spoons of soup in the dining room before he begged off and asked to be wheeled on his cot back to his bedroom.

I went into the front room, happy to find it empty, and sat down. For awhile I stared at a picture on the wall of Christ blessing the children.

"You're very quiet." The doctor's ability to slip unnoticed into a room was uncanny.

"Just thinking, Dr. Carlson."

"Evelyn." She sat down next to me, a small tidy woman of sixty, deep wrinkles in her face, short gray hair. "I wanted to ask you…" She hesitated. "What happened to you in church today?"

I looked at her aging face—kind, honest, warm—and I found myself telling the whole thing. Amazing. Ben Sylvester, Mr. Independence, spilling his guts to a stranger, hoping she would understand, maybe even accept me.

When I was done, I said to her, "I think he told me that it

was time for him to act, now that I've decided to trust him. Our situation's about as impossible as it can get. What better time for him to—"

"How do you know he promised to rescue you now?" she asked.

"He told me. It stands to reason…" I hesitated.

"Ben, you said some words to him. He responded. But when did he give you the opportunity to prove you can trust him?"

"Do you doubt he can save us?"

"No. All I can tell you is that he usually doesn't make it that easy. Could we pray? Could we thank him that you've come back to him?"

"Why are you doubting him?"

"I'm not," she said.

When she prayed for me then, her words weren't sentiment. They were like discovering the meaning of life after you'd thought it had blown away in the wind. Maybe she didn't interpret my vision the same way I did, but she knew the one who had given it.

Kdoma slept until a couple of hours past nightfall. When he woke up, he seemed much stronger, though the comparison didn't mean much considering how terrible he'd looked the last time we'd talked.

When I explained to him what had happened to me in the church, he brightened. "I had been praying, Ben. No man can carry such a burden as you were bearing. To look at yourself as the one who has driven God away and has put his family at risk—that is not what any man should endure."

"None of us will escape this unless we trust him," I said, testing my ability to say such things out loud, the words coming hard.

"We must trust," Kdoma said, but his eyes flickered away from me.

"I have news," I said. "Murphy's dead."

"How do you know?"

"The radio. They say the coup's been contained, except for a few renegade troops who are running for the borders."

"Do not believe all you hear," Kdoma said.

"Some of the leprosy patients came over here about an hour ago." I paused, not knowing how to break it to him. "The hospital compound is surrounded by soldiers, probably rebels, about sixty of them."

Kdoma looked grim. Even though he was somewhat prepared for it, the reality seemed to hit him hard.

"They probably don't know you're a federal agent," I offered.

"They will know. Governor Saluso will be coming here."

"You can't be sure of that."

"If he is alive, he knows his only hope is to find a suitable hostage, and he also knows where your wife has been and where you are going. Why do you think we have sixty soldiers circling the compound? If they wanted to overrun us, they could have done so hours ago."

"They're afraid of the leprosy patients," I said.

"Perhaps. But I doubt that any fear of lepers would hold them back for long. They are waiting for the governor to arrive and give them instructions."

"What about you? If Saluso finds you…"

"Then I will die," he said. "Slowly."

"I'm sorry. If you hadn't taken me to find my family, you'd be safe with the president by now." He said nothing, turned his head. "Kdoma?" He wouldn't look at me. "I'm sorry," I said again.

"No, I am the one who is sorry." He looked at me, stricken. "I have told you that I was disobeying orders by taking you to your family. Perhaps in some ways I was. But my journey was an opportunity for me."

"Opportunity?"

"I knew that Governor Saluso would either die or be captured in the attack on the army base, or he would escape. If he escaped, then he must needs be captured. So I left evidence along the way so that he would know where we had gone and would perhaps come after us."

"What kind of evidence?"

"Wherever we stopped to buy food or petrol, I told them I was a federal police officer fleeing Governor Saluso. He will follow us to within twenty miles of this place, and then he will find us here."

"Why did you do it?"

"I knew he would want revenge and he would need hostages. Perhaps I hoped…" He paused.

"You used us as bait so you could nab Saluso."

He smiled sadly. "How ironic it is that I would be disabled just when I need to be the strongest."

Ironic. We were in the middle of a journey to nowhere, without any evidence that my family would ever be found.

And now Kdoma, flat on his back, had lured Saluso right to us. If God was going to do what he'd promised, now was the time.

CHAPTER SIXTEEN

BEN

"Get up!" The shout smacked into my heart with such force that it bolted me upright before I knew I was awake. Men. Men in uniform. Guns leveled at my face.

I tried to remember where I was and somehow connect with the nightmare in front of me, but it took more effort than I could muster. The guns were rock-steady, all aimed right at me, faces of the soldiers like granite. I'd been in bed asleep.

"Who are—"

"Silence. Lie on the floor." Eight soldiers in green uniforms plus a captain. All of them looked grim, their uniforms dirty and torn. They filled the small bedroom.

They searched me roughly, then the room, tearing apart everything in the process.

"To your feet." I stood. My knees nearly betrayed me, but I managed to steady myself against the wall. "Go to the other room. Not too quickly." I walked into the front sitting room. The others were already there—the doctor, Kdoma on his cot.

"Are you all right?" I asked Kdoma.

"Be quiet," the captain said. "You are having no rights here."

I was awake enough now to take a closer look at him. The man was tough through and through, no hint of weakness anywhere. His men were a motley crew, but they had guns and we didn't.

I sat next to the doctor, who looked completely unruffled. She'd probably seen just about everything during her years in Africa.

They were waiting for something. No one needed to guess who was going to walk through the door next. When he came in two minutes later, it was an anti-climax. Saluso, looking like thunder, the fury on his face more than compensating for his insignificant physical form. He was still in his quasi-uniform but it was now none too clean.

Songo Saluso stared hard at Kdoma lying on the cot, incapable of defending himself. "Take this man outside and kill him," Saluso said, his voice calm, as if he'd asked a servant to clear away the dishes after a meal.

The captain reached over to Kdoma and grabbed one arm. Another soldier the other.

"No!" I said.

"Why are you speaking now, Ben? This is not the season for the white man to rule the black." Saluso's eyes looked glazed. "Captain, take this man outside and kill him."

"You can't mean it," I said.

They did. They dragged Kdoma outside, and a few seconds later there was a single shot.

It wasn't real, of course. This wasn't happening. I was still asleep at home in my bed in Lynden, Washington, where people didn't burst in with guns and execute other people on a moment's reflection. But the illusion wouldn't work. I'd heard the shot and I hadn't done anything to stop them from killing the man who'd saved my life. I should have rushed at Saluso's throat, but I stood rooted to the floor.

"How in God's name could you do that?" I managed.

"I did not do it in God's name," he said. "I'm not sure I have to be believing in God any longer. You can see from the failure of my dream that I no longer have any God to thank."

"You just killed a man."

"A man who ruined my life, who perverted the destiny of my people."

"Who made a fool out of you."

He rushed over and stood inches from me, his face a blur. "I will no longer tolerate your insolence, Ben. Nor will I tolerate any resistance to my orders. My killing of Kdoma was intended to assure that from you."

"What orders? You lost the coup. They're hunting you down as I speak, and you've got nothing left."

"I have you. And the doctor here."

"Hostages?"

"It lacks imagination, but yes. Hostages. At this moment up to a hundred soldiers still loyal to my cause are circling this compound. More are coming every hour. We intend to win safe passage to _____." He named a neighboring country.

"How do you know they want you there?"

"I am not a fool, Ben. We made contingency plans long ago."

"And just how do you plan to get all of us out of here? Some kind of truck convoy?"

"That is my concern. It is not yours." He turned and spoke to the captain, who had returned while we were talking. I didn't hear what he said, but the captain motioned to his men and left the room.

"So it was all your scheme right from the beginning," I said. "Murphy was only the bag man. What did you do—kill him yourself?"

"A shell caught him while we were running to the truck. I cannot deny that it has saved many problems for me."

"You know, Governor, I almost started to believe in you when you showed me your village and introduced me to your spiritual father. It turns out my first instincts were right— you're just a shabby little snake."

"Life is never that simple, Ben. There are few truly evil geniuses in this world. Most of us have our reasons."

"And yours are?"

"I care about my people. Have you any understanding of what has happened to them since the oil came? We used to have small industries, a chicken in every pot as you Americans say. But the oil took precedence and everything else faded away."

"Your country is rich."

"That is incorrect. Our rulers are rich. Our people are poor. The rulers have stolen their livelihood, even their dignity."

"Well, you've certainly been flaunting your own wealth," I said.

"A show. A ruse. If I lived in self-induced poverty, the rulers would have known I was dangerous."

"Come on, Songo. You and Murphy were such idiots that everyone knew what you were planning almost before you did."

"I warn you, Ben." He looked angry enough to hit me.

"Don't bother warning me, Songo. Just tell me what bizarre plan you've got lined up this time."

"The plan is mine. You have no part in it except to obey me." He turned to the doctor. "We will need beds for the evening for myself and the captain. The others will be staying in the forest."

"There are a few spare beds in the leprosy hospital," Dr. Carlson said. "I'm sure you'll find it comfortable."

"My warning extends to you, Doctor," Saluso said. "At this point, I intend to leave you here alive when we depart. But if you wish to be a hostage, I can arrange it quite easily."

"Let's cut through all that, Saluso," I said. "You're done for. Why don't you just recognize it?"

"I am the one with the soldiers and guns. You speak like a fool."

The rest of the day was a sorry thing—rainy, all of us stuck in the house, none of us keen on conversation. Saluso sat in an armchair and read an old *Reader's Digest,* no sign of guilt for his many crimes on his smug little face.

There was lots of time to think, something I didn't welcome at all. The fear that I'd lost Karen and the kids, the shock and horror of Kdoma—none of it was good grist for my mental mill. At least I knew I wasn't alone. After the events of the past few weeks, I'd never again think of God as a crutch for weaklings.

Saluso's psychological state was complex, and I needed to start figuring it out. There was no question that he knew he'd lost the coup and had to leave the country. If he was captured, the best he could hope for was to die fast. Like Kdoma. He was under amazing stress and he had a Messiah complex—a bad combination. I couldn't appeal to his faith, because he'd never really had one. At one time I'd been his jinx. Hurt me and God wouldn't let him win his coup. But that was probably gone now too. All in all, my only hope was to do exactly what he said.

His soldiers were a concern. I doubted they could all escape with Saluso, but had he told them he was going to leave them in limbo, to the mercy of the troops loyal to the president? I hardly thought they'd be amused at the prospect. As it was, the federal troops would probably be all over us soon anyway. Would the fact that the doctor and I were hostages hold them off, or would they come in with guns blazing anyway?

"There's healing for our fears, Ben," Dr. Carlson said, watching my expression.

"He told me he'd act," I said, wondering whether Saluso was really into his reading or already trying to figure out my meaning. I felt myself clutching at a mystical experience in a leper church, time starting to blunt the edges of memory, the old Ben Sylvester clearing his throat in the wings, waiting for his cue to march on stage.

"It might take time, Ben," she said.

"It won't. There isn't any time."

"Please be quiet," Saluso said, looking up from his magazine.

"No, you be quiet," I answered him, as if we were brothers quarreling because we were bored and it was raining.

Then it was 4:03 in the afternoon. I'd just looked at my watch for the hundredth time when there was a commotion outside, people shouting. Before Saluso could go to the door, the captain burst in and started whispering in Saluso's ear.

"Bring him in," Saluso told him. The captain went out and brought back an African sergeant, very rugged looking, his uniform dirty and torn, a stranger to me. Without a word, the three of them went off into one of the bedrooms. Whatever it was the sergeant had come for, Saluso looked worried, and from the bedroom, I heard him shout something about "too many of them." Most of the rest was unintelligible. Then, as they came out of the room, he said to the captain, "All right. Bring them." When he glanced at me, his look was calculating.

I wasn't ready for what was about to come through the door, even after the experience of the leper church. The door opened and they led a man and woman in, white, in their early thirties. I didn't know them. And behind them—I can still feel the shock now—behind them were Karen and Jack and Jimmie.

Jimmie shouted "Daddy!" and flung himself at me. Karen stood there, as amazed as I was, then ran to me and embraced me. I looked around for Jack. He stood a few feet away, his face covered with tears. I motioned him to join us, and he rushed over and threw his arms around me.

"How?" I couldn't even find the words to ask her.

"Not now, Ben," she said, crying. "Are you all right? Please tell me you're all right."

"Yes. You? The kids?"

"We've had a very bad time, Ben."

"You're not hurt? Did anything—"

"We're fine now. You're alive."

For a few minutes, nothing interrupted us while we absorbed the fact that all of us were alive. Finally, Karen introduced me to Tom and Kelly, then Saluso broke in, "That is enough of sentiment. Sit down." His eyes darted back and forth among us. "Sit down!"

We sat. "Why don't you tell our visitors what's happening here, Governor," I said.

"There is no need."

"Tell them how you've made us your hostages. The governor here wants to save his skin, and we're going to be his pawns."

"Ben," Karen said.

"This is a failed coup attempt," I said. "There are loyal soldiers breathing down our necks, the woods are full of very scared rebels, and Saluso here does not intend to be captured."

"Governor?" Tom asked him. "Is that a fair assessment?"

"It's filled with misunderstandings, but the result would probably be the same. I intend to leave this country, and I will need some travel companions who can guarantee my safety."

"You're going to take all of us?" Tom asked.

"No. I shall have to make a choice at the proper time."

"What about your soldiers out there in the jungle?"

"I am not sure I appreciate this inquisition." Saluso put on a scowl. "If you are truly needing to know, my soldiers understand the importance of my survival if our cause is ever to be realized."

"Translation," I said. "He's saying that he intends to leave his merry men to their fate while he goes elsewhere to regain support for another coup attempt. Those soldiers out there are going to be chopped liver, but at least they'll suffer and die in the glad knowledge that their leader is safe."

"Ben. Please." Karen had a warning tone in her voice.

"My path out of the country will bring me much risk as well," Saluso said. "I cannot take all those soldiers nor do I need all of you."

"Maybe you should just choose your other alternative for dealing with people you don't need," I said, thinking of Kdoma.

"A plague on you and your house, Ben!" Saluso shouted, suddenly furious. "Come along, captain." The two of them left, taking the sergeant with them.

Karen then told me her story—fleeing Tom and Kelly's home, getting captured by the rebels, losing all the army vehicles and most of the rebel soldiers, the despair when they saw the broken axle and realized they were isolated in dangerous territory.

"We went to a local village," Karen said. "The sergeant had only three men left, but he bullied the people and made them feed us and house us. In the morning, he made us walk. The next night was the same thing—another village, more bullying. Then this morning…" She paused as if trying to organize the memories. "This morning we met another rebel troop. We were afraid they'd fight over us, but it turned out that the two sergeants were old friends. The other sergeant told us that the best place to go was this leprosy hospital because the rebels were reorganizing here. We went back to Tom and Kelly's van and drove it here. Seventy miles of bad road and nobody tried to stop us. Do you know how amazing—"

"I know," I said.

"But it was so horrible. If it hadn't been for Tom and Kelly…"

"Thank you," I said to them. But I couldn't hold back my rage at Saluso. This should not have been happening, and that little creep was to blame for our agony. I forced my fury back down. Calm yourself, Ben. Now is not the time for stupidity.

There was a pause, then Karen asked, "What's Kdoma doing here?"

"Kdoma? Saluso…" I hesitated.

"What, Ben?"

"Saluso had him executed."

"When?"

"Hours ago."

"No, he didn't. I saw Kdoma outside when we came in. He's lying on a mat in the courtyard."

"Are you sure he was alive?"

"Of course I'm sure. He told me he was sorry we hadn't escaped the country."

"Maybe it was someone else."

"Ben, it was Kdoma."

CHAPTER SEVENTEEN

BEN

Ben!" I must have heard Karen screaming at me to stop, but I was out the door, my eyes darting around for just one sight of Saluso, seeing him, rushing him, wallowing in rage for all he had done, my hands ready to grip his throat if I could get close enough to shake the life out of him. He turned, there in the courtyard, and the terror stood out on his face for the second before the captain lunged and hit me in the side of the head.

I went down hard, my thoughts scattering. "You're a fool, Ben Sylvester." No, it wasn't Saluso speaking to me. It was me, telling myself what I already knew. When was I ever going to get it right?

I heard Saluso shout, "No, Captain!" I turned my head, seeing boots beside my face and above them a hand with a pistol in it pointed at my head. If it hadn't been for Saluso's order, I would have been shot on the spot.

"Get up," the captain said, his voice showing weariness and disgust.

As I pulled myself upright, I saw Kdoma, very much

alive, lying on a mat in the shade of an overhanging roof. He was looking at me with an expression of surprise.

"You're alive," I said.

"In the flesh," he answered. Then Saluso rushed me and shoved me into the wall of the house. Karen was standing in the doorway, too frightened to speak. The kids hung behind her.

"I have too many hostages as it is, Ben," Saluso told me fiercely, his eyes glittering with fury. "Perhaps you and your family would like to leave this life and go to be with the God you love so well. I could arrange that in an instant."

"Why not? You've already put us through hell. And what kind of a man are you pretending that you killed Kdoma?"

"Would you rather that I had truly killed him? I needed to disarm some of your foolish bravado."

"So why didn't you kill him? You must hate him mightily, and there are lots of hostages to go around." He didn't answer, just walked away from me.

"Go inside," the captain said. "We will not have any more of this trouble from you."

When I went back into the house, Karen said nothing about my attack on Saluso. The others were there, wanting to know what was going on, looking concerned when I told them.

As soon as I explained about Kdoma, Dr. Carlson went outside without a word, and a few minutes later they brought Kdoma back in and put him on his cot. There was a light of triumph in her eye.

"Are you all right?" I asked as we wheeled Kdoma into the living room.

"Better now," he said. "I am too sorry about the deception. There was no way for me to inform you that I was still living."

I moved his rolling cot near the large sofa. It was time to put some strategies together while our enemies were outside.

Tom asked the first question. "Ben, are you sure Saluso's in control?"

"Sure I'm sure," I said.

"He had a chance to kill Kdoma, a man he despises and doesn't need as a hostage, but he didn't. He could have killed you just now, but he didn't. Has he killed anyone for the cause of his coup?"

"Murphy maybe. I don't know."

"Maybe he doesn't have the nerve to kill anyone."

It was worth considering. Maybe all westerners with a faith were jinxes to Saluso. Maybe he still harbored a fear that God would get him if he harmed us.

Kdoma explained what he knew of our situation. While the federal soldiers would probably be careful about risking so many westerners, they had to capture the governor. Letting him flee the country was no good because his rebel soldiers would fight on to preserve their lives, and Saluso could easily become some kind of god to whoever survived.

Right now, the federal army was mopping up the rebel base in the north, but they'd soon be on their way after Saluso. Already they'd dedicated a couple of jets to harassing rebels in the territory around us.

"So how does Saluso plan to get out of the country?" I asked.

"It would have to be a chopper," Tom said. "Any kind of ground transport would take too long and face too many chances of being stopped. And a plane can't land here. No runway."

"Where would he get a chopper?" I asked.

"Not locally, or it would probably already be here. Maybe from whatever country's promised him shelter. I suspect he needs to get clearance from Mtobe's government for a chopper to fly safely into the country and back out again."

"Why would anyone give that man shelter?" Kelly asked.

"It has happened before," Kdoma said. "In Africa, countries will often have jealousies or border disputes. I have in my mind two countries on our very borders that might enjoy humbling us by giving shelter to the governor."

Just then, Saluso and the captain came in demanding their supper, and the doctor went off to arrange for its preparation. Saluso glared at me but didn't say anything.

Karen and I spent the evening getting the kids settled down. Jimmie was fine, but Jack continued to brood. Deep inside him I could sense fear and anger, but he wouldn't talk about it. I only hoped there wasn't any permanent damage.

After the kids were in bed, Karen and I spent a couple of hours together sharing our experiences, trying to get in touch with some kind of foundation in the middle of this chaos. I told her everything, including the way I'd caved in to Saluso. She cried, more, she said, because she hadn't been there to walk through it with me. I sensed she was angry that things had turned out so ugly for us. Angry at God or at me? Didn't she understand that God was getting set to bail us out of Mtobe?

We slept badly and both of us woke up feeling grouchy. The doctor's housegirl served us breakfast. I don't remember what it was. None of us was paying too much attention to food.

A waiting game had started. Hour after hour passed while Saluso stayed somewhere outside, giving us no information, leaving us to speculate about our future. Soon we started getting on each other's nerves, the kids driving us to distraction with their boredom. At least the waiting gave me time to assess Tom and Kelly, and I concluded that we could count on them if things took a turn for the worse. I only hoped they could count on me. I scarcely trusted myself.

What was it about this life with God that was so much of a struggle? Karen had been so steady and assured, but now she was angry. I'd been given a rare vision, but the old Ben Sylvester was already fighting to emerge.

It wasn't until mid-afternoon that anything happened, but then it was sudden. A jet flew overhead, incredibly low, earsplittingly loud. No warning. He must have come almost straight down on us. Jack burst up from his chair, screaming something I couldn't hear. Jimmie buried himself in Karen's blouse, and she curled up in a ball over him. The rest of us were in shock, covering our ears with our shaking hands.

The jet was gone after one pass, leaving behind a high-pitched whine in our ears. Jack sobbed quietly on a chair at the edge of the room.

"A message from our president no doubt," Kdoma said. "He wants the governor to recognize that we plan to be the victors because we have the power."

"He's not planning to invade the hospital, is he?" I said. "We're hostages here. How committed is he to saving our lives?"

"My president is a man of great learning and gentleness. There is no question that he will be doing his best to save our lives." I'll bet, I thought.

About an hour later, we heard a small helicopter landing and feared the worst—that Saluso had arranged for transportation and we were about to be carried off who knows where. Instead, Saluso brought in a stranger perspiring in a black suit with knotted tie. The man, an African, was in his forties and had a look of officialdom about him. "As you see," Saluso said to the man, "they are all here and safe. Are you satisfied?"

"Yes." The man spotted Kdoma and went over to him, smiling broadly. They talked in their own language for a few minutes before Saluso became impatient.

"Please return now to your masters," he said to the man. "I do not intend to prolong this negotiation." Saluso led the man out again, their voices disappearing into the courtyard.

"Who was that?" Karen asked.

"One of our people," Kdoma said. "From the president. He says they are negotiating about the governor's escape from the country, and he has a firm offer to take back to the government."

"Do you know any details?" I asked.

"No."

"How long will it take?"

"I am sure they are having radio communications with

the president. The decision will not take a long time."

Sure enough, when it was almost dark Saluso came back in looking triumphant. "They have agreed to all of my demands," he said. "We will leave at dawn."

"Exactly who is leaving?" Tom asked.

"There is space for everyone in this room."

"I wish to stay here," Kdoma said softly.

"You will come with us."

"I am a member of Mtobe's security forces. Do you know what they will do to me in the country you are going to?"

"It is a condition of our departure," Saluso said. I realized, suddenly feeling sick, that there were better ways of getting revenge than taking a man out and shooting him. Whatever country was going to shelter Saluso would love a real live security officer from Mtobe, someone who could be forced to tell them all about Mtobe's defenses. Kdoma was facing a horror beyond anything I wanted to think about.

"I'm of no value to you," Dr. Carlson said suddenly. "My place is here with my patients, and your men here may need medical attention."

Saluso looked at her, calculating, then nodded his head. "You may stay."

"What about your men, Songo?" I said. "Are you leaving them behind?"

"They are soldiers. They know how to obey orders."

"Have you told them they're being abandoned to the mercies of the president's forces?"

His eyes went cold, and without warning he turned and left the house. I dreaded to think what these rebels might do if they found out before we got away.

Night, and it was harder this time to get the kids to sleep. They knew we'd be moving out at dawn. Jack seemed afraid to shut his eyes in case he experienced the nightmares he'd had the night before. He kept looking at me with intense fear, even after I explained to him that God was about to save us.

When they finally both went down, I looked across at Karen through the muted light of the bedroom. "I'm so sorry," I said. "This should never have happened."

"It's not your fault."

"Who's fault is it?" She didn't answer. "You have to understand," I said, "that I trust him. I wasn't stringing Jack a line."

"What if he doesn't help us?"

"He will."

"What if he doesn't, Ben?"

"You weren't there in the church."

"I was ducking bullets and comforting our children." Her voice was edged and she brushed her hand against one of her eyes.

"What's happening to you, Karen?"

"It shouldn't have been this way. He's not in charge anymore."

"You're alive. He's going to act."

"How do you know that?"

We went to bed uneasily. I'd never known her to doubt God this way. Sleep came hard.

Finally it was dawn. We heard the helicopter from our bedroom, coming in low, a big machine judging by the rushing beat of its rotor. The captain brightened up the morning by bashing on everyone's door and shouting that we had to be ready in ten minutes. There was to be no luggage, only what we were wearing.

We dressed quickly. Ever fickle, Saluso announced as we came out of our rooms that he'd decided to take the doctor along too.

A half-hour after waking we were rushed into the single-rotor Sikorsky S-55, army issue, sparse, hard seats, too noisy for conversation. Funny—I'd built a plastic model of the thing when I was a kid. They'd brought it out in the early 1950s, and it was unique for its engine in the nose and its shock-absorbing undercarriage.

I looked at Karen sitting across the aisle from me with the kids. She smiled at me weakly. Jack and Jimmie were tense, quiet, not even thinking of enjoying the novelty of their first ride in a helicopter.

Then Saluso and the captain got on, Kdoma hobbling between them in pain. The other soldiers, what we saw of them as they came out of the woods, seemed to be just waking up. They looked surprised, and as I watched them certain lights started going on for me. If Saluso hadn't told them he was abandoning his fair country, there was no telling how they would react when they figured it out.

I wanted to warn Karen, but there was no real way to protect ourselves if things got ugly. Once we were seated and strapped in, there was nothing I could do but look out the small window beside me. Saluso was at the door, and I could see him arguing with the sergeant who had brought Karen to the leprosy hospital. I couldn't hear what they were saying, but it didn't take much intelligence to recognize what the fight was about.

Other soldiers joined the debate, something unheard of, I suspect, in the rigid hierarchy of an African army. Then someone went back into the woods and came out with a large machine gun, and when Saluso saw it he retreated hastily inside the chopper. With a lunge, the captain shut the door.

Suddenly we were airborne, and the rebel soldiers still on the ground backed off because of the noise and the flying dirt. Then I saw the soldier with the big gun raise it to his shoulder. He hesitated, unsure of whether or not to commit an outrage. We were going up fast, and I knew he was going to shoot.

Bullets started banging into the thin shell of the chopper. Across the aisle I could see Karen sheltering the kids, all of them screaming at me, but I couldn't hear them. Bullets were blasting through the fuselage all around us, the skin of the chopper offering no protection except for the floor, which must have been armored. The pilot swung us into a fast circle and went horizontal, zigzagging enough to bring our stomachs to our throats, and the bullets stopped hitting us as we moved out of range, trying to climb. We were only a few hundred feet up.

But it was too late. The rotor above us started thumping out of rhythm like a Model T Ford in need of a tune-up, and then the chopper suddenly nosed downward. The pilot tried to keep it level while the rotor thumped away, the engine in front sputtering, revealing mortal wounds.

Crash positions. I saw Karen showing the kids how to put

their heads between their knees, not knowing what good it would do when we hit the jungle. The chopper was tilted now at an impossible angle, and I couldn't reach Karen and the kids. But I could see her shouting at me "Ben!" even if I couldn't hear her. We couldn't tell each other the things we needed to say and hear before we died.

CHAPTER EIGHTEEN

BEN

We were all hunched over, kissing our knees, when a sudden jolt flung us against our harnesses, bashing us up against the metal shell of the chopper. Alive. Slowly we uncurled and looked around, surprised to be breathing, while the chopper motor continued to stutter, as if the thing might try to take us up again.

We'd come down on a back road, missing trees on either side by inches. The pilot must have been a genius. There we were in the middle of a dirt track, prim and upright, the only sign of trouble the faltering sound of the rotor. Then the engine shut down, and there was nothing but our accelerated breathing.

"Is anyone hurt?" Saluso asked.

"What do you care?" I said wearily, unstrapping and going from person to person, checking on everyone starting with my family. I ignored the captain. Everyone was fine except Kdoma, who was still in no shape to be bashed around the inside of a falling chopper. He tried to mask the pain, but the sweat on his face betrayed him.

"We need somewhere for Kdoma to rest," Karen told Saluso. "Whatever you think of him, Governor, you can't be cruel enough to let him suffer like this."

"It's not up to Saluso," Tom said softly. "He's not in charge any more."

"Yes I am." Saluso reached over to his confederate. "Captain, your pistol." The captain gave it to him. "Now, you will be doing exactly what I tell you."

"Or you'll shoot us? Get real, Songo," I said. "With your own men out there hating your guts for running out on them? How far did we get—ten miles? Put the gun away so we can discuss how to survive this."

Karen looked at me, her eyes pleading with me to keep my big mouth shut. Evelyn took her medical bag, which she'd somehow managed to keep, and started working on Kdoma's leg, checking the dressing.

"How is it?" I asked.

"No bleeding. I'll give him something for the pain."

"Make sure he is awake and alert," Saluso said. "I do not want this man being a liability to us." Three cheers for the milk of human kindness. What a hero Saluso had turned out to be.

We'd been in the chopper for about ten minutes since we landed. The heat and humidity made breathing a problem. Saluso finally told the captain to open the door, and we braced ourselves to face whatever was out there.

A whole village of Africans had gathered along a tree-lined road with paths leading off it to homes and farms. In front of us were about two hundred people, standing silently, impressed by our sudden arrival out of the sky. Their leader was easy to spot—a small man with almost white hair, unusual for senior Africans who usually colored out the gray.

Somehow they already knew who we were. Maybe they recognized the governor. The chief of the village lost no time making his position clear.

"You should not have come here," he said, in English for our benefit. "We are loyal to our president, and you will bring trouble on our heads."

Saluso waved the gun vaguely in his direction and said loudly, "These white people are my prisoners. It will be much trouble for you if I am compelled to shoot one of them."

I had no idea what his plan was, but I'd seen enough of Saluso not to underestimate his ability to think up nifty schemes on short notice. I couldn't figure out how the guy could continue to be so cocky.

"We will need a car," Saluso went on. "A five passenger car in good condition. It must be a taxi."

That was no problem. Taxis were normally everywhere. With rebels loose in the woods, they'd stopped operating, but they were readily available. A five passenger car—what was the guy up to? The villagers had one brought over within fifteen minutes, a battered Peugeot that, like most taxis in the country, sneered in the face of regular maintenance.

"This is what we will do," Saluso said when everything was ready. "There are too many hostages for comfortable passage from here. In a few minutes, we will be leaving with Ben, Kdoma, the doctor, the captain, and myself. No one else."

"You can't do that," I said. "Anyone you leave behind will

be at the mercy of the rebel soldiers."

"You have become tedious, Ben," Saluso murmured softly. "I am very tempted to shoot you and take one of the others. Clearly I have failed to cause you to understand the importance of my work. It grieves me. And so, even though I despise the impudent using of your tongue, I relish the time we will have to speak together." Megalomaniac talk.

"You're insane, man," I said. "Where do you think you can go now?"

"You know far better than to be asking such a thing in front of all these people."

"What about my wife and children? These other people?"

"We will care for them," the chief said. "No one will harm them. I pledge that to you." For some reason I believed him. But I scarcely dared look Karen in the eye.

"We'll be all right, Ben," she said. "Please do what this man tells you." She gave me a brief smile. Jack looked horrified, Jimmie just frightened.

"The pilot," Tom said. "Are you going to leave him too?"

"We have no room for him," Saluso answered. "If we are able to hide the helicopter, perhaps he may repair it and make his escape."

"There is no place to hide a machine of such great size," the chief told us.

"Of course there is," Saluso shouted. "Push it under those trees."

But the rotors were too big, and even with the whole village pushing, they only got it halfway concealed.

"When the federal air force sends their jets up," I told

Saluso, "it will take them no time at all to find that monster. They'll hunt you down pretty quick. Give it up."

"Get in the car!" Saluso was bellowing now, panic in his eyes. "All of you get in now!"

"Forget it," I said. Saluso raised the pistol and pointed it at my left eye. "You're nuts. This isn't supposed to be—"

"Get in now or you will die."

Evelyn and I, supporting Kdoma, moved toward the car.

"The captain will drive. You will sit in the middle of the back seat, Ben. The doctor to your right. Get in now!"

We set off in an easterly direction, toward the border, the car lunging around the first corner almost before I could turn for one last glimpse of my family. I saw them for a second, staring after me. Then the battered taxi took us out of sight.

"Go back!" I shouted. "I'm not leaving them again. Listen to reason, Songo."

"Steady, Ben," Evelyn said. "Don't be foolish." Saluso and the captain ignored us.

"You don't have a chance," I said. "Give it up." Like talking to a wall.

We were moving fast for the narrow dirt road, the captain trying to put away as many miles as he could before the air force found the chopper. But heading for the border was ludicrous. It was the first place the president's forces would look for us.

About five miles along, Saluso said to the captain, "There. That appears to be a possibility." A branch road angled off to the left. We took it, heading north. What was going on? A couple of miles along, we swerved off onto a road pointed northwest. "Yes, that's it!" Saluso shouted.

"Where are we going?" I asked. We were now headed deeper into Mtobe, north and west of the leprosy hospital. Every mile was taking us farther from the border.

"Be silent," he told me. There was something about the fire in the look he gave me over the front seat that told me I'd reached the end of his tolerance and more so.

We drove. Fast. Dangerously. Each of us knew a road-block just had to appear around the next corner. But Saluso must have been dusted by his fairy godmother. We went on and on with no opposition until, an hour along, a jet flew over us, low and loud. There was no way he couldn't have seen us.

"Stop the car!" Saluso shouted and the captain immediately did what he was told. "Kdoma and I will be disembarking."

"Don't be ridiculous," Evelyn said. "The man can't even walk without help."

"I will help him. Get out, Kdoma. Hurry. The jet is returning."

We were opposite a small farm in the bush, just like the hundreds of others that had dotted our route. Saluso got out, then helped Kdoma out, making a show of paying off the captain as if he and Kdoma had taken a real taxi ride and the captain was the taxi driver. Then the two of them walked toward the farm, Kdoma leaning on Saluso, his gasps audible through the open window. To the jet that flew over again, it looked like we'd just delivered a couple of passengers.

Without any hesitation, we drove off, leaving Saluso and

Kdoma behind. No doubt Saluso didn't even know the people who lived in the farm he was visiting.

"In case you had prepared any plans, Mr. Sylvester, I must now remind you that I have the gun," the captain said as he drove.

"You've left your master behind."

"I am not a fool. We will hide ourselves and return for him after darkness."

"There are roadblocks after dark," Evelyn said.

"We have plans for that, doctor."

The captain ran out of words, so we moved on in silence for a few more miles to a stretch of road that was heavily forested. We drove under the trees as far as we could without bogging down in swampy ground.

We spent the day there, mostly not talking, while I watched the trees for snakes. I'd heard they hang around up there, waiting to slide down on the unwary. Maybe the ugly yellow of the taxi scared them off, because I didn't see any. No one, of course, had brought food or water, so we were all pretty far gone by the time darkness fell just after six and we started back for Saluso.

We almost didn't find the right house. It took three passes and a few arguments before we located the place for sure. Saluso came out, confirmed who we were, then went back and got Kdoma.

"Help them," the captain told me.

I got out and tried to absorb as much of Kdoma's weight as I could while Saluso came up behind carrying a sack and a large water jug. Easing Kdoma gently into the car was no mean feat, but I don't think I hurt him too badly. The doctor slid over beside him and started checking his condition. Saluso put the sack in the trunk, got in the front passenger seat, and told the captain to get going.

"We need food and water," Evelyn reminded them after a few minutes. "Can't we stop?"

Reluctantly, the captain pulled over under a large tree and shut off the lights. It was a rough picnic—chunks of bread, corned beef from a can, bananas. Miraculously, Saluso had rounded up a six-pack of the universal beverage—Coke—so that we wouldn't have to risk drinking the water. I guess dysentery wasn't welcome in his taxi.

We started off again, and it wasn't half an hour before we came to our first roadblock—a log thrown across the road, men with kerosene lamps standing around. These weren't police, just local citizens trying to protect their neighborhood.

"Doctor," Saluso said.

Evelyn got out and talked to the men. Without much hesitation, they pulled the log aside and let us through. Smart. With a British doctor along, we had safe passage almost guaranteed. All she had to do was show her identification and announce that she was on her way to an emergency up ahead.

But it wasn't an easy passage. No matter what bush road we took, we got stopped at least three times an hour. After awhile, it all became surreal, like a dream sequence in some obscure Italian movie. With our murky passage through a world dominated by darkness and waving lanterns, it was like a whole new civilization had emerged with the setting sun, the world turned on its head.

Saluso was in a serious panic by the time the sky started to brighten. We hadn't gotten far enough, and he had to find a foxhole for us. Near the equator, night turns to day in twenty minutes. Still, Saluso found someone he knew before the sun hit us. We drove up to a house and the man took us in, hid the taxi, gave us a corner to sleep on mats, fed us when we woke.

The next three nights were repeats of the first except that Saluso became talkative and regaled us for hours with his vision for his land and his people. What a thrill it was to hear him. By the fourth night, we were all exhausted, but at least we'd moved too far west for squads of rebel soldiers to be lurking around. Because of our cover of darkness, the air force hadn't found us either. As near as I could tell, we were headed back either to Saluso's home in the state capital or to the village where he'd grown up.

I'd been praying again, almost constantly. If the helicopter was as visible as it seemed to be where it came down, the federal people would have found it within hours after we crashed. Karen and the kids would have been rescued and put under the president's protection. At least that's what I was praying for. I couldn't think of any other scenario that I could live with.

"I'll rescue you, Ben," God had said. "All I wanted was that you repent and give me your all." Thank you very much. This was the finest rescue I'd ever seen.

At the end of the fourth night, just before dawn, we turned onto an especially rough track. As soon as I felt the car rocking under us, I knew what our destination was. The open field with the big stone church in the middle of it confirmed what I feared.

And it suddenly made sense to me with a clarity that amazed my worn out, fuzzy mind. Saluso knew he didn't have a chance. With the crash of the chopper, any possibility of escape was eliminated. So he'd come home to make peace with himself or pull off a last stand or do some other crazy thing guaranteed to risk the lives of his hostages before he went out in a blaze of glory.

Saluso was a desperate man with nothing to lose.

CHAPTER NINETEEN

BEN

The stone church rose out of the gloom, massive, stable, a contradiction to everything that was sure to happen in this place. We were fugitives and hostages, blundering into a village where we did not belong, bringing the terror with us, putting everyone there at risk.

My anger at Saluso had grown mightily in the past hour. It was bad enough that he had plotted a botched coup and taken captives. But to bring it all home with him, into the place where people adored him, where his spiritual father must by now be feeling the knife of betrayal in his back—that was more contemptible than I could have imagined.

We drove across the wide open compound, no sounds but our car and a few barking dogs. I half expected Saluso to complain that there was no welcoming committee, no cheers of adulation for the failed hero.

They were awake, though. As we parked near Reverend Craven's house, they started coming out of their houses, curious at the early arrival of a car from the outside. Saluso got out and waved to them. There was no answering cheer, not even rumbling conversation in the growing crowd, only silence.

Saluso found a dirt mound nearby and stood on it.

"My friends," he shouted, "never have I been more happy to be in my home." This in English, though there was no need for it. I suspected he wanted to sound official, to leave the impression that he hadn't lost everything. English belonged to the world out there, to government and bureaucracy.

"You have no doubt been hearing many things concerning the events of the past few days. Many are saying that I attempted to overthrow our duly elected government. They are saying that I committed such an outrage out of bitterness. But I want now to reveal the truth of this tragic situation.

"I have been a great victim. I trusted the man Murphy, this man who has been revealed as the slave of the oil companies. I believed in him for a time, just as we always seem to be believing the white man. Your governor has been a fool. This man Murphy plotted an insurrection of monumental evil, and through great duplicity, he has made me the public figure at the head of it. I had no suspicion until the bombs started to fall."

It almost worked until the crowd parted and an old man, white, with white hair, walked forward and stood beside his son. He turned to Saluso, and in the growing light I saw that his face was covered with tears.

"Songo," said Craven. "You should not have come."

"I am here now. Are you going to send me away?" Saluso's voice was soft.

"Why do you feel you have to lie to us?"

"Lie?"

"To tell us stories about the man Murphy and your ignorance of his plans. Did you think we are only simple folk so that we'd accept whatever you told us?"

"My father, I cannot believe that you would accept the fabrications of the western news services instead of my own word."

"At one time your word had value. Not any more." Craven turned away and walked through the crowd, leaving Saluso speechless. I watched Songo's face as it went through surprise then confusion, then recognition, and finally dismay.

He stepped down from the little knoll he was standing on and walked over to me. The crowd watched him, silent, staring.

"Are you preparing to gloat, Ben?" he said to me, as if he was surprised that his phoniness was so obvious to everyone.

"You live a lie and you die a liar," I said. "How are you going to make it right with them? They used to think you were a hero."

"Not a hero. I simply desired to bring their dreams to life. I wanted to help them, that is all it ever was."

"You wanted power, Songo." I didn't care anymore what his aspirations were. There was nothing left in me but exhaustion.

"We must talk, Ben."

"That's all we've been doing. How can you still think you have something to offer to these people?"

"Is it all so plain to you? Did you ever truly try to understand me?"

"I'm a political scientist. I've met people like you all over the world."

The villagers were losing interest. Gradually they faded away, their faces tight, their eyes angry, leaving only us five—Songo and me and the doctor and Kdoma and the captain. Kdoma, unexpectedly, had perked up considerably during the past few days and could even walk a few hundred feet by himself. Now he leaned against the car, listening to the conversation.

I was fed up with conversation. Only two things concerned me now—how to get out of Saluso's clutches before he got us all killed, and how to get my family and me out of Mtobe. The latter was out of my hands for the moment, but I was prepared to work hard on the former. There was no way I wanted to be a sacrificial lamb for Saluso's blighted cause, and God didn't seem to be showing much desire to lend a hand.

"May we speak together?" Saluso's face had a childish expectancy to it. What in the world was there left to talk about?

"No," I said. "I'm tired. Where can we sleep?"

"Reverend Craven has extra beds. You and the doctor should be going there." His voice was tired, disappointed.

"Kdoma comes too."

"All right."

We walked to the cement house where the aged missionary was waiting for us at the door. "I am so terribly sorry, Mr. Sylvester," he said, his eyes red.

"What for?"

"I told you to trust Songo. I was convinced he was the victim of Mr. Murphy."

"He fooled all of us. Don't worry about it."

"There was a time when he wanted only the good of his people."

"I know," I said. My sense of reality was flattening with my growing tiredness, three dimensions squashing into two, no depth of thought or feeling left.

He got us bedded down, the doctor in one bedroom, Kdoma and me in another. In no time I fell into oblivion. It was afternoon before I surfaced again. Four-thirty by my watch. Night after night of tense travel had taken the stuffing out of me, and I knew I'd need more sleep soon.

First, I had to get together with my fellow hostages and Reverend Craven, if he was in the mood for talking. Kdoma lay in the bed next to me, dead to the world. I dressed quickly and left the bedroom. The doctor and the missionary were already up and sitting in the living room.

"Was the bed comfortable?" Craven asked, a sad smile on his face.

"Great," I said. "I hope you didn't think I was being unsociable. My body just stopped working."

"Not to worry. Dr. Carlson here has been explaining your situation. Do you have any idea why Songo came here?"

"Have you ever heard of David Koresh or that cult in Switzerland?"

"You can't mean some sort of suicide pact?" Evelyn said.

"Maybe. Saluso's journey started here. He's come home to die among his adoring fans. Maybe he plans to call on his admirers to make a grand statement by dying with him. Or maybe he has some notion that he can reboot the coup from here."

"He must be very lonely," Craven said. "That man had such dreams when he was younger. Where did it all go?"

"Somewhere along the path from folk hero to power seeker he lost it," I murmured.

"I've disgraced him. I denounced him in front of his own people."

"Regrets?"

"Yes. It's hard to accept that someone I thought I knew has become a stranger. Someone I love dearly."

"Better that he hears it from you than that he leads this whole village into disaster."

Evelyn sat forward. "What options do you think we have now, Ben?"

"I don't know. Presumably Saluso has some confidence that we won't wander off. I think he knows I'm not going to leave Kdoma, and the poor guy's not even good for a quarter of a mile yet."

"Your thoughtfulness is touching." Kdoma limped into the room and sat down heavily. "But for now we need to think more of contacting my people. Are there any communications devices in the village? A ham radio?"

"No. Nothing," Craven said.

"Have you seen any army forces recently?" Kdoma asked him.

"They're here now. Encircling the village. They're federal troops, not rebels. Arrived about two hours ago."

"What?" the three of us said in unison.

"It means nothing. From what the doctor has explained to me, the federal soldiers are unwilling to risk your lives in an invasion. They'll wait."

"Will Saluso?" Evelyn asked. There was no answer to that one.

"Do you have sufficient food for everyone here in the village?" Kdoma asked.

"Yes. And our wells are filling with the rains. We can survive for weeks without outside support."

We ate supper together and spent the evening in small talk. None of us except Craven were keen on more sleep just yet. He stayed up late with us, ever the gracious Englishman.

It was about ten when the jet flew over, low and loud. Déjà vu. No one could mistake the message—the African version of "Gotcha," the federal troops telling Saluso he didn't have a chance. It killed the conversation handily.

Outside nearby the avengers had gathered, fully prepared to quash the final vestiges of the rebellion. The loyal soldiers were ready for action, and the target was Saluso. We westerners were worth something, so they wouldn't do anything sudden and risk the wrath of our home countries, but I wasn't ready to take any comfort in that. Saluso could do us all in through some crazy scheme or other, and I had no way of measuring the patience of the federal troops.

Eventually we drifted off to bed. I remember praying, but not with profound words. The terrors of our dilemma didn't call for eloquence. Most of all I kicked myself for believing God was going to do something dramatic. He seemed to prefer watching to acting. I slept badly.

Morning. We'd spent twenty-four hours without seeing Saluso's face or hearing his voice. That was worth something. But I woke with the conviction that I had to find out what the man was planning to do, why he had brought us here.

As soon as I could, I went out and started wandering around. Villagers stared at me, but with no overt hostility. At the edges of the large clearing were the houses of the inhabitants of this place, and beyond that the jungle. But I could see no sign of the federal troops, nor did the people I met seem overly worried.

A sudden rainstorm hit, and I ran for shelter to the church, the door unlocked, the stained glass windows letting in very little light because of the darkness of the clouds. This was the place where Saluso had made his plea to me for understanding when he first brought me to his home village. It now seemed long ago.

"It is very dark today."

The voice startled me and I whirled. Up there in the pulpit was Songo, his face just poking out above its massive structure.

"I didn't realize you were here." A church was not a welcome setting for a heart to heart with Saluso.

"This place is a sanctuary," he said. "Where else should I be?"

"So…" I said, at a loss.

"Why do you hate me, Ben?" It was the voice of a child, plaintive, peevish.

"I don't hate you, Songo. On the other hand, I don't respect you either." What did he want from me, adulation? Or did he want me to tell him that I despised the ground he walked on?

I couldn't really say what I thought of him, because I hardly knew myself. The closest I could come was that he seemed like just another nickel and dime would-be potentate ready to sacrifice any scruple in the quest for power. People like that didn't need to be hated, just shunned.

"I wanted you to understand me."

"Why?"

He didn't answer. I looked up at him, and he was weeping, the tears barely visible in the gloom, but definitely there.

"Sorrow for your losses, Songo?" I said.

"Losses happen often in life, Ben. It is harder to accept hatred from a man who should have understood you."

"Me? Why is it so important that I understand?"

"Because I am not what you believe me to be."

"What are you?" I was having trouble keeping the disdain out of my voice.

"I am an African. Why do you white masters find it so difficult to see our aspirations?"

"So this is a white man-black man thing?"

"Can you not see that the people of Mtobe need their own identity, apart from the control of white men?"

"I think I do understand. You really did want to get rid of Murphy, didn't you? You manipulated your whole plan with me so you could put him out of the picture."

"He would have made me a slave. I am not a slave."

"And you were going to nationalize the oil?"

"I do not have to explain what I was going to do. What you must understand is that no white man will rule Mtobe."

"Neither will you."

"You people give us your education, your medicine. You teach us that the supreme goal of the African is to worship at the shrine of the American. Then when we defy you, you declare us to be ignorant savages."

"Don't be ridiculous."

"Would it help if I worshipped you?"

"What?"

"If I came down from this pulpit and fell at your feet?" He came down the steps and walked down the aisle until he faced me, two feet away. Then he slowly sank to his knees and dropped his face to the floor.

"What are you doing?"

"What we always finally do, white man. You give us your God and your ways, because ultimately all you want is that we love you."

"Get up! This is ridiculous." I wondered if I was going to be sick. He stayed motionless. "Get up, Songo!" I grabbed him by the shoulders and hoisted him to his feet. "What in heaven's name are you talking about?"

"It's what you want to believe, Ben." His face was wet. "You people bring us your superiority and you actually think we should make it our highest goal to win your favor. We listen to your pious talk and watch your far better ways, and then you expect us to imitate you in everything, as if we were slaves, not a people with dignity or with dreams."

"You're misunderstanding me, Songo."

"Who are you, a white American, to be passing judgment on me?"

"You've betrayed your country and people have died. You put my family in danger, lied to us, almost got us killed. Hasn't any of this gotten through to you?"

"This country is your idea, you haughty people from the West. We did not create this place Mtobe. It is your democracy, not ours. And your oil money has destroyed us."

"It made you rich."

"Only some of us. Only those seduced by the corruption. It has made the rest of us into paupers."

"How?"

"We had industry, commerce, self-sufficiency. But when the world is desiring your oil, nothing else matters anymore. Let everything else of value go to ruin. We have oil! Who can be concerned that all the wealth is falling into a few greedy hands while the industries that would have helped us have collapsed? We have oil."

"What does this have to do with me?"

"It has to do with your arrogance, Ben Sylvester. You have great understanding of what a worthless revolutionary should look like, and you hate what you see. Why should you take into account my dreams, my self-sacrifice, my desire to rescue this exploited people? You recognize my kind, and they are dirt under your feet."

"There were other methods open to you. It didn't have to come to treachery and bloodshed."

"Is that obvious to you?"

"What about your faith? Would Jesus have taken your way?"

"It is your faith, not the faith of the African. Your faith would tell us to be meek and kind, never to be using force to rescue a people from poverty and exploitation. Your faith would keep the African in subservience forever, with a smile on his face."

"That's not true. If you had even an inkling of the Gospel, you'd know how wrong you are."

"The African is always wrong. That is why the missionary came to us."

"Reverend Craven raised you, educated you."

"Do not believe that I am ungrateful, Ben. But the love of one white man does not compensate for the evils done here in this land in the name of helping the poor African to rise out of his darkness."

"What about the Jesus you said you trusted once?"

There was no quick answer this time. He stood for a moment, blinking, then looked at the floor. "That is the loss I regret the most," he said.

B E N

hat are you going to do?" I asked him.

"Whatever I must do." Saluso's face was like carved ebony.

"You know that the federal troops have circled the village."

"Yes."

"You don't have a chance."

"There is always a chance." He looked at me as if I were a child who still couldn't understand something everyone else already grasped.

"We need to know what you're planning," I said, my voice revealing tension. "Come on, man, you've got our lives on your hands."

"Have I killed any of you? Have I even hurt any of you?"

"Don't get self-righteous on me again," I said. "I want this to end. You've played with us long enough."

"But it is not time for an ending yet, Ben. You think like an American."

"You're surrounded. The rescue chopper is gone. Even

your fellow villagers are tired of you."

"It is truly a shame that you are such a limited man, Ben. I preferred the description Mr. Murphy gave me of you before I had met you."

"What—the man who can be bought?"

"He pictured you as an adventurer. I had many hopes that you might understand my vision and realize that even now it is far from dead."

"Are you planning a remake of Custer's Last Stand?"

"Custer? Oh, the American soldier who brutalized the natives and then foolishly let himself be slaughtered. Do you really believe I came here to find death?" He walked across to a window depicting Christ blessing the children. "Do not ever underestimate me, Ben."

I left him then. If not a death wish, then what could it be?

The rain had stopped, but I had to dodge the puddles as I walked across the clearing. I had no destination in mind. What Saluso had said was nagging me, and I couldn't concentrate on anything else.

The man's bravado was amazing. After all the duplicity and nastiness, he still made it look as if the white man was the bad guy. But I couldn't put it past me. He'd called me arrogant, and somehow it had stung.

Karen was always telling me that I wrote people off too quickly. She talked about the way Jesus hung out with the dregs of society and worked to drag them out of the pits they'd dug for themselves. Could Saluso be worth a second look?

Not on your life. Just thinking about Karen and what

Saluso had done to us made my blood race again. But to my surprise, though I tried to hang onto it, I found the anger slipping away. I started thinking about Saluso's tears, that stunt with the bowing and scraping. He wore his righteous indignation so well. Why did he keep getting to me?

I completed a circle of the compound and went back to Craven's house. Kdoma had found a stick somewhere and was using it to help him walk around the yard. He limped badly, and there was pain, but he looked stronger.

"You training for a marathon?" I asked him.

"Not nearly that kind of distance. Just past the village and into the woods."

"What?"

He paused and gave me a steady look. "Tonight I intend to contact my people."

"Saluso will shoot you if he finds out. Besides, what good will it do? Your people already know we're here."

"I want to be sure they do not kill you, Ben. Some elements in our army are overzealous. They are probably calling for a full invasion." He walked another dozen yards, his forehead wet.

"I just spoke with Saluso," I told him, having no trouble keeping up as he hobbled along.

"What did he have to tell you?" Kdoma's tone was measured, showing restraint, but I could feel the undercurrent of contempt.

"When we first arrived, I thought he'd come here to make some kind of last gesture and then die in a hail of bullets. But now I suspect he still thinks he can survive this."

"How? He has lost his support even among the people he knows best."

"I don't know. But the guy is crafty."

"I will warn my colleagues when I see them." Winded, he sat down on a step at the front of the house.

"How far can you walk?"

"Perhaps a mile. I intend to leave just after dark and return by morning. Obviously the governor believes I am still weak or he would be guarding me more properly."

"The governor has other things on his mind. I wish I knew what he was planning."

The rest of the morning passed slowly. I told the doctor about Kdoma's intention to contact his people. I didn't tell Craven. The man had too much power in this village, and I didn't want him getting a notion that Kdoma's enterprise might be counterproductive. To me it sounded like Kdoma might be able to do some good, at least to call off the hawks among the loyal forces before the whole place got mortared.

I decided to try to get myself into shape. Who knew what I might have to do before this was over? So I walked around and across the cleared compound again and again, occasionally having to find shelter from the rain.

It gave me a good chance to think. For some inscrutable reason, God had backed off on the assurances he'd made to me. A test so he could watch me snap? Some grand game even bigger than Saluso's? Whatever it was, he'd left me in limbo again as if he really wanted me to take things back into my own hands.

I wondered where Saluso had gone after our talk in the

church. Was he meeting with the village elders, trying to regain support? Or had he found some way to communicate with the outside?

Twice while I walked, jets flew over. Both times I took cover, holding my ears. I had no idea whether or not they'd start strafing. They didn't, but clearly Kdoma's people wanted to keep the pressure on.

It was cooler now, the clouds more predominant than the day Karen and the kids and I had arrived scarcely three weeks earlier. I barely worked up a sweat as I walked. But I wasn't ignored. Every second I was under scrutiny by some person or other. White people this far in the bush were still a curiosity.

I wondered how Craven had managed all these years. The isolation was almost palpable, though I suppose he'd gotten so deeply into life here that eventually it felt as if the world ended where the jungle circled the village. The people probably scarcely thought of him as a westerner anymore.

Noon. I went back to our quarters and shared a meal with the doctor, Kdoma, and Craven. All of us were growing edgy. How do you live like that—in constant dread that forces outside your control will wipe you off the map? Is there a special grace for menacing times?

After lunch, Kdoma snagged me into meeting with him in a cool spot under some trees. The doctor found us after a few minutes and joined in. I could tell that Kdoma was a bit spooked about the run he was planning that night, but I didn't want to give him too much false hope.

"Don't be so sure no one's guarding us at night," I told him. "Just because you don't see anyone watching the place during the day doesn't mean Saluso hasn't rounded up some followers to watch the place after dark."

"What followers?" Kdoma asked. "Where are they?"

"Your life's at stake, Kdoma," Evelyn said. "We don't want you taking risks that can be avoided."

"It's my duty to reach my people."

"Then let us help you," I said.

"Do you have a plan?"

"An idea." I told him and was surprised that he liked it immediately.

Darkness. The long afternoon had done none of us any good. One more flyover from the air force. Tedious hours of waiting. We'd decided not to tell Craven that Kdoma was planning to bolt.

Ten o'clock. Craven had gone to bed when I quietly opened the front door and walked across the yard and down the trail toward the central clearing where the church was, making sure I could be seen, a small kerosene lamp dangling from my hand, lit. A hundred yards from the house a figure loomed out of the darkness, a flashlight suddenly turned on, shining in my face.

"It is late, Mr. Sylvester." The captain.

"Who can sleep?" I said. "I keep thinking about the danger we're in."

"It is not safe to be walking in the darkness."

"I have my lamp."

"The governor has asked that you and your associates be remaining indoors at night." His tone was firm and final. I walked back, my eyes searching the darkness for signs of other watchers.

Once inside, I whispered my findings to the others. "The captain is along the trail to the central compound. I spotted movement at the right and left corners of the house, in the front."

"What about the back?" Kdoma asked.

"Who knows?" I said. "Look, Kdoma, it's too dangerous. If they catch you sneaking off, they'll probably kill you."

"Would you be willing to help with a diversion?"

"Like what?"

"You and the doctor. Perhaps you could improvise? But there is no time for rehearsal. You must make your performance now."

I looked at Evelyn. "You game?"

She smiled back at me, pulled me toward the front door, and shoved me outside onto the porch with a surprisingly loud shout of indignation. "Get out of this house!" she raged at the top of her voice. "If you have nothing better to do than complain and criticize, you can sleep in the church." Her acting was impeccable and her voice loud enough to wake the dead.

"Are you crazy?" I yelled back. "Look at reality. We're all dead people and all you can say is 'Let's be nice to each other.' Why can't you see that we've got to do something?"

She shouted back and I answered in kind, watching out of the corner of my eye as the captain approached up the trail and the watchers near the house came out to have a look, including a man who must have been lurking by the back door until his curiosity drew him to the commotion at the front.

"Silence!" the captain said, command in his voice. "Go

inside. I have no interest at all in your petty squabble. Settle it among yourselves. Go inside at once!"

We faked some awkward looks at each other and did what he told us. My view of Evelyn Carlson had risen a few notches.

Kdoma was gone as I expected, out the back door and off on his journey to contact his compatriots, leaving us with nothing to do but try to sleep despite our fears for him. Craven hadn't come out of his room, though he must have heard us. I prayed for Kdoma, hoping it would matter, trusting it would.

Finally I slept for awhile, coming to just before dawn, looking across at Kdoma's bed which in the darkness seemed occupied, though I knew it wasn't. Had he made it through? Who knew how many followers Saluso still had in this village who might have waylaid Kdoma before he could get to his people?

By the time daylight came, I was sure Kdoma had bought the farm. Craven commented on the gap in his guest roster when we sat down for breakfast.

"Kdoma must have over-exerted himself yesterday."

I sighed. "No, he didn't. He went out last night to make contact with his troops."

"And didn't return."

"He told me he'd be back by morning," I said. "We need him."

"Is that your only concern?" Craven asked. "That the man is useful to you?"

"Of course not. He saved my life. Maybe I saved his. I care what happens to him."

"Perhaps his superiors prevailed on him not to come back here," Evelyn said.

"Maybe." I finished breakfast and went out. Something drew me to the church again. I opened the door and let it shut behind me, standing quietly while I waited for my eyes to get used to the darkness.

"I have been waiting for you," a voice said. Kdoma's voice. He was sitting in the shadows on a pew near the front.

"You're all right." I walked up the aisle for a closer look.

"It was too dangerous to re-enter the house with all the guards in place. I slept here for a few hours, waiting for them to go to their beds. Presumably it is safer now."

"None of us were sure you'd come back."

"I am responsible for you," he said.

I sat down at the end of the pew and drew my feet up on the seat. "What's the news?"

"Your family is safe." He heard my gasp. "How ironic it is," he went on, "that after all our efforts they should be saved through the crash of a helicopter."

"Where are they?"

"In a hotel at the capital. Our soldiers found them soon after the accident."

"Will they be sent home if anything happens to me?"

He frowned. "Of course."

"And what about your soldiers out there?"

"They were going to invade at dawn regardless of the consequences. I have convinced them to wait for another two days. As it happens, I'm not sure this was a good thing. It appears the governor has a two-way radio—a very good one."

"Where did he get that?"

"My suspicion is that it was in the helicopter. It seems he has contacted someone from outside the country. Our soldiers received only the end of the transmission, but they heard the words *helicopter* and *hostages.*"

"He's going to try it again? The same plan?"

"Apparently. He must get out if he wants to save his life and have any hope of regaining influence in Mtobe."

"So this nearby nation thinks Saluso's valuable enough to go to all the trouble of a second try at rescuing him? They've already lost a chopper and a pilot."

"They're not just receiving Governor Saluso. They are receiving me. As you know, I have a great deal of knowledge of my nation's secrets."

"So Saluso is using you as a bargaining chip to attract his rescuers."

"The other portion of his transmission that we received was a single sentence: 'I have the intelligence officer.'"

"Saluso said that?"

"Yes." Kdoma seemed to be taking it calmly.

"You came back to us knowing this, knowing that you're going to be hauled off and tortured until you tell this other country everything you know?"

"The safety of Dr. Carlson and yourself is now my primary task after my need to capture the governor."

I gave him a close look to see if he was joking. He wasn't.

"Come on," I said. "Let's get you back to the house."

No one paid much attention to us as we walked across the clearing. I guess they were starting to get used to our presence.

As long as they hadn't seen Kdoma leave during the night, they wouldn't think he was returning from anywhere except a walk with me around the compound.

We got him fed and bedded down, Craven looking at him with concern and suspicion, but asking nothing. Later I filled Evelyn in, but we still didn't include the missionary.

I was tempted to confront Saluso head on, especially about his plan for Kdoma. But I didn't dare risk revealing that I knew what Saluso was scheming. He might take it out on Kdoma, suspecting the truth that Kdoma had contacted his superiors.

So I let it ride and waited, chafing, realizing that we had only two options, both of them nasty. Either someone would show up with a helicopter, or the federal troops would invade by dawn the day after tomorrow.

Later I went for another long walk around the compound, ducking a couple more cloudbursts, trying to pray but finding it hard to put the words together. Once a jet flew over, low, loud, grating on my nerves as I flattened myself against a house.

When I got back to Craven's house, Kdoma was up.

"We have to plan this," I said.

"What must we plan?" He looked tired.

"Saluso's only leverage here is his hostages. Without us, your troops would move in right away."

"Do you have some magical power to cause us to vanish?"

"We could go out the back door like you did last night."

"Ben," he said, "why are you continuing to strive?"

"Is there an alternative? In case you've forgotten, you're

due to be taken to another country and tortured before they kill you."

"I haven't forgotten." He stood with the help of his stick. "Walk with me." We walked in silence to the clearing, then along its perimeter.

"Ben," he said after a few minutes, "I have been watching you for many days."

"And?"

"Why do you carry the entire world upon your back?"

"Because no one else will."

"Not even the one who made it?"

"You mean the one who disappears whenever I need him?"

"What task do you need him to perform?"

"Our rescue. What else?"

"Your wife and children are safe. If the helicopter had not crashed, how do we know that my army would not have shot it down before it crossed our border?"

"And kill all those westerners?"

"You must understand how seriously our government views the danger of Songo Saluso. As well, I carry many secrets."

"They were going to shoot us down?"

"That is not something I wish to answer. I am only telling you that you seem most willing to tell our Lord what is a true answer to prayer and what may not be."

I said nothing.

"Every one of us," he went on, "every one assumes that God is only needed when we reach the end of our resources.

Then when we finally give our lives to his care, we berate him about the nature of his answer."

"Don't you know you're doomed, Kdoma?" I said. "What are you going to do about it?"

"There is nothing left to do," he said.

"We could try to escape."

"There is no further means of that. Can you truly believe that we will be able to deceive our guards a second night?"

"Could I try to reason with Saluso?"

"Try as you will," he said. "What I need, however, is someone of faith who will pray."

When everything called for desperate action, I couldn't understand why he'd given up so easily.

CHAPTER TWENTY-ONE

BEN

The real problem now was Kdoma. The man had saved my life. He'd shown constant intelligence, courage, devotion to duty. More than that, I felt a bond with him that went beyond anything he'd done for me. We were brothers, servants of a common Lord. I wasn't ready to see him sacrificed and myself walk away with my life.

Troubled, I slept that night, old dreams of terror, pain, and accusation hovering at the edges of my vision, longing to be reborn. Even in my sleep I knew I couldn't give in to them, not if I wanted to avoid the pit constantly opening at my feet. There was a path through this, a genuine one with sure footing and protective railings around it. Stay on the path, my mind told me.

Morning, and I didn't wait for breakfast. It was time to find Saluso and make the pitch of my life.

I walked through the large clearing in the semi-light. People were up and about, but no one I asked knew where Saluso was. Most, I could see, couldn't care less. They gave me looks that spoke volumes of their desire simply to be rid of the man.

I found him in the church, alone, up there in the pulpit again.

"Are you preparing a sermon?" I asked.

"Just say what you must and leave, Ben. I find you exceedingly tiresome." His voice sounded hollow.

"It's obvious what you're planning," I started, not knowing anything for sure.

"And what is that? What plan?"

"Another helicopter. The doctor and I will be hostages. Kdoma will be carrion for the lions."

"You have become very perceptive. How did you learn about this?"

"I'm right?"

"Of course." He looked at me as if I were stupidity personified. "You have always underestimated me."

I took a deep breath and said, "You need to modify your plan."

"How?"

"Let Kdoma go."

"He is a large part of the arrangement. Letting him go is out of the question."

"Do you know what they'll do to him?"

"Have you not seen what he has done to me?" Sudden rage in his voice, his eyes shining. "For a year I trusted him as I would a son."

"Revenge must be sweet for you, Songo," I said.

"Do not be patronizing me, Ben. Who gave you the role of judge?"

"They'll turn him into mush and then he'll—"

"I am well aware of the destiny of fallen spies."

"And you've got no feelings left for him?" I walked closer to him, so that I had to tip my head back to see him. I wanted to study his eyes, his expression, to see if there was any chink in the armor he'd constructed for himself.

"It has been my desire, Ben, to keep you alive, and your family alive, and the doctor, and even Kdoma. Can you not understand that life puts realities in one's way which simply are unavoidable?"

"You could surrender."

"And then my people would go on suffering. You may think I am motivated only by revenge in Kdoma's case, but I have no desire to have the man suffer. The captain and I could have wounded him painfully or even killed him long before now if I only wanted to punish him for destroying our movement."

There was no reason to go on with this. The man had no intention of sparing Kdoma.

"Pray with me," I blurted.

"What?"

"You say you have no desire for revenge against Kdoma. Surely then you can pray with me about his fate."

"You know that I would not do that."

"Why? Because you're in a state of mortal sin?"

"I have abandoned the western God. He is no friend to the African."

"Kdoma finds comfort in him. All I can see is that you're afraid of him."

"Go away, Ben."

"Let me pray then." I had no idea why I repeated this. It was like an intrusion into my mind that wouldn't rest until it was expressed.

"You do not need my presence in order to pray for the traitor." His voice was louder.

"Let him pray, Songo." The voice came from behind me, the voice of Reverend Craven. "Please. We are speaking of the destiny of a man who was only trying to serve his country. Let Ben pray."

"After you have condemned me in front of my own people, why should I want to obey you any longer?"

"Because you are still my son." Craven walked out of the shadows and I saw his tears. "Nothing you do will ever change that for me."

"Do not think me ungrateful for all you've done for me, Father, but I cannot return to the days when I was a little boy who you tucked into bed after my prayers were completed."

"That little boy had faith in God."

"He was naive."

"Please, Songo, let him pray for Kdoma. Surely you have no pleasure in the man's death."

I thought Saluso would order us out or walk out himself, but suddenly he gave in. "All right. It means nothing in any case."

This was something I had no experience doing—leading an invocation to God for the life of a man about to die.

"Come down here, Songo," I said. To my surprise, he came down and stood squarely in front of me. I started to pray.

"Lord," I said, not closing my eyes, looking at Saluso's face, "I pray for Songo, who has forsaken you. He's trying to escape so that he can live to fight another day. Lord, show him the right path."

Saluso's mouth tightened, and I thought he'd put a stop to it. For the first time I noticed he had a pistol stuck in his waistband. I moved on quickly.

"Kdoma, Lord. Personally, I don't believe it's right for one of your children to suffer and die like he's going to. Be near to him, and I pray he won't experience much pain because of the power lust of Songo Saluso."

Saluso's cry of rage confirmed that he'd agreed to let me pray only because he couldn't bear to hurt Reverend Craven any further. But I'd pushed it too far. I put my hand in front of my face as Saluso slowly pulled the big gun out of his waistband.

"Is it right, God?" I shouted. "Does Songo have your blessing to destroy a man who was only doing his duty?"

The bullet should have ripped through me then, but nothing happened. I was too terrified to look at him. I shut my eyes and left my hand where it was. Slowly, I said to him, "Kdoma's blood is on your head. Do what you have to."

"And may God have mercy on my soul? Is that what you want to say, Ben?" His voice was unusually soft.

"Yes." I opened my eyes and dropped my hand. He stood there, the gun held loosely at his side, his face showing confusion.

"Do you hate me?" he asked.

"No." It was pointless to ask him again why it meant so

much to him. He'd tried to explain it to me. I just didn't understand. "I'm sorry," I said.

"For what?"

I didn't answer him, just turned and left the church, brushing past Reverend Craven, not looking at him.

Back at the house, I told Kdoma all of it. When I was done, he gave me a grim smile and said, "I have been trained for this, Ben. I am grateful for your help, but do not fear for me."

He wasn't trained for this. No man is trained for humiliation, torture, and death at the hands of people who don't care.

In my mind I kept repeating the words, "May God have mercy on your soul." But Songo Saluso couldn't hear me.

CHAPTER TWENTY-TWO

BEN

One-forty in the afternoon. The thump of the rotor coming in fast from the north chilled me in the heat of midday. For the past couple of hours the captain and his associates from the village had taken up their posts around Craven's yard. Houdini couldn't have found a way to escape from there.

The helicopter landed somewhere near the church, a bigger and newer Sikorsky this time, two jet engines whining at an ear-piercing pitch. The captain rushed into Craven's house, grabbed Kdoma with one hand and me with the other. "You two," he said. "Quickly!"

"What about them?" I asked, looking at Evelyn and Reverend Craven.

"Leave them! Come with me!"

"What can we do?" I said to Kdoma as the captain rushed us toward the chopper.

"We will trust," he said.

"How can you just give up?"

"If there is a chance, I will take it. If there is not, I have God."

"Silence!" the captain said.

Saluso stood by the church door, dressed in a black suit. Who had he robbed to clothe himself so well?

"Into the helicopter!" the captain bellowed, fear obvious in his face, his eyes wild.

"No!" shouted Saluso. I could hardly hear him as he motioned us toward him. "Come into the church!"

"What are you doing?" the captain yelled. A soldier armed with an automatic rifle had come out of the helicopter and stood by its open side door, his gun pointing at the ground. Inside the machine, I could see four or five other men in green camouflage, probably armed the same way. Still gesturing, Saluso directed us into the church.

"What's the delay?" I asked. "Do what you have to do."

Saluso stared at me thoughtfully, as if we had all the time in the world.

"What are you doing?" I repeated. "Loss of nerve? What? In case you haven't noticed, we're in danger here."

"Be quiet, Ben. Kdoma, tell me what your superiors plan to do with us when the helicopter takes flight."

"If you are an intelligent man, you will already know the answer to your question," Kdoma said.

"Tell me."

"No."

I knew the answer too, and I'd been using the past two hours to make peace with myself, with God. Kdoma had finally decided to explain it all to us, there in Craven's house: "If they allow the helicopter to land, my forces will launch an attack and try to rescue us. If the helicopter takes us into the air, they will shoot it down."

Saluso had miscalculated. For one thing, his hostage pool was far smaller now than the first time he'd called in a chopper, and now it didn't include any children. For another, while the federal soldiers would have liked to take Saluso alive, he was better dead than plotting against the president from a foreign country. Finally, Kdoma knew too much about Mtobe's secrets. His people would never let him be taken alive and tortured.

I hoped I'd made myself ready enough to die. Not easy to do when I knew God hadn't kept his promise in the church. Maybe he'd never even made a promise and I'd been nursing a figment of my imagination. My family was safe. Maybe that was enough for him. One thing was sure—if this was the end, I'd go to my grave still trying to figure him out.

"Tell me," Saluso said again.

Kdoma stared at him. "Why should I tell you? Do you not understand that you are a traitor to your country and to your tribe?" He spoke slowly, and I suddenly realized he was stalling. The federal soldiers needed at least ten minutes to move in on the clearing.

But a ground invasion would be tricky in the extreme. The clearing was at least three hundred yards wide from the jungle to the chopper, and open ground would make a dandy killing field if the soldiers in the chopper opened fire. What was more, the chopper would block the federal troop's view of us if we came out of the church and tried to board.

Someone banged on the church door, probably the captain, desperate out there as he waited for us.

"Tell me," Saluso said again.

Kdoma was never going to tell him, and Saluso was smart enough to have figured it out anyway. We'd waited too long already. Blame it on Saluso's crisis of nerve. Maybe Kdoma was trying to pressure him into surrendering, but of course Saluso couldn't expect any more from Kdoma's people than that they'd suck him dry of the information about his dealings with the oil companies. After that, execution.

Saluso opened the church door and motioned us out. The sun, uncharacteristically, was shining, and I found myself blinking at its harshness. I was surprised that I felt little emotion.

Saluso walked ahead of Kdoma and me, the captain behind us, pistol drawn. I glanced at Kdoma and he flashed me a quick grimace as if he was trying to communicate something to me. Together we walked slowly toward the chopper, limited by Kdoma's limp, which seemed more pronounced than it had been. Ahead of us, Saluso turned and angrily motioned us to hurry.

Fifty yards to the chopper. The soldier standing in the doorway of the machine raised his rifle to his shoulder, pointing it in our direction.

I imagined Jack and Jimmie growing up with only faint memories of a dead father, the little family shrine on the mantle with a picture of Dad in his best suit.

Twenty yards, and I saw the federal troops bursting out of the jungle directly across from us on the other side of the chopper. The soldiers inside the helicopter—I could see them plainly now—were facing the wrong way, watching the four of us approaching. My heart started to race until I realized that their inattention had been only a momentary lapse.

Someone in the chopper shouted, and all five of them, except for the guy pointing his gun at us, turned and started firing out the side windows of the helicopter at the advancing soldiers.

Federal soldiers, right out in the open, started dropping. The ones still on their feet fanned out.

Everything was moving in slow motion. I stopped, unable to move my legs, watching a war from the front row, losing all hope.

Kdoma, coming up beside me, stumbled and fell to his knees. I was afraid he'd been hit. The captain rushed up from behind us and bent to pick up Kdoma and drag him toward the chopper. I whirled and smashed the captain to the ground with a blow that sent a flaming shock up my arm.

Kdoma scrambled to his feet, grabbed the captain's gun, gave me a "come on" gesture, and tried to run toward the church. I could see he'd never make it. The soldier at the door of the chopper was aiming at us, and the only obstacle in his way was Saluso, who had stopped and turned toward Kdoma and me. Amazed, I watched Saluso pull his pistol out of his suitcoat and point it at us, holding it with both hands in a shooting stance. And then I was running, scooping my shoulder under Kdoma's arm and dragging him toward the church, feeling his weight slowing me down, weaving as bullets began to smack into the ground around our feet.

Noise and confusion and running and the church was too far away, forever too far. I was propelled forward by a heavy concussion in my right leg, coming to earth too fast, too hard.

It ended there.

CHAPTER TWENTY-THREE

KAREN

I t was mid-afternoon of the next day when the Mtobe air force flew Ben to the hospital in the national capital. Karen asked for him to be moved back to the States, but the American ambassador told her they had a specialist who was very good. Her memory is quite clear about that.

The bullets had broken Ben's upper leg, torn some ligaments, ripped some muscles. There might be nerve damage. The surgeon would have to put a pin in and reattach all sorts of things. No one could tell Karen with any certainty whether or not he'd walk again, but at least he was alive.

It was Kdoma, then, who saved him, dragging him into the church and getting shot himself in the fleshy part of his shoulder as they went through the door. What this man had risked and suffered for Ben and Karen could never be repaid.

The hospital staff wouldn't let Karen see Ben until after the operation, but she was able to visit Kdoma in a nearby ward. His bullet had gone right through his shoulder without hitting bone. He looked very bright despite all that he'd endured. That strong face and those clear and honest eyes were wreathed in a smile of welcome.

"I am sorry, Mrs. Sylvester," he said right away. "I was trying to protect him." It was only later that she learned he had escaped from the village a couple of days before the battle but had come back to help the hostages.

While he sat up in the hospital bed he told Karen everything about that last day, right up to the final moments. He told her about the desperate attempt to escape, Ben risking his own safety by trying to help Kdoma to run. She could hardly bear to listen anymore.

"When the bullet struck Ben," Kdoma said, "we both fell to the ground. I looked back at the governor, and his pistol was pointing at us. The captain was only starting to rise after the blow Ben had given him."

"So Governor Saluso shot Ben?" she asked.

"Yes. When he fell, I began pulling him toward the church. Then someone shot me as well, whether the governor or the captain I do not know. Later, after the fighting had ended and I had stopped the blood flow from Ben's leg and my shoulder, I looked out and saw that the helicopter had burned."

"And Saluso?" she asked.

"Burned near the helicopter. The captain as well. It appears they were engulfed by the exploding of the fuel tanks."

"Both of them are dead?" she asked. "You're sure of that?"

"Yes."

Kdoma must have seen her shudder.

"I wish to know how you are faring, Mrs. Sylvester. And your boys."

"We're all right," she said, thinking of her worries about Jack. "Sometimes I feel angry."

"You have every right for anger," he said. "My country has not received you as it should receive its guests."

"I think I'm more angry at God than at Mtobe."

He stared past her at the opposite wall for a moment, and then he said, "Our Lord answered all your prayers and saved your lives."

"He put us through absolute horror, and Ben might be in a wheelchair for the rest of his life. Do you call that an answer to prayer?"

"When you called him Lord," he said, "you agreed to let him set forth your destiny. He gives us the best, not the worst."

"This is the best?"

"It is only our humanity that causes us to question him."

"I can't accept your explanation," she said, close to tears.

"If we raise our fist against the God of adversity, Mrs. Sylvester, what God can we find to replace him?"

From the corner of her eye, she saw a nurse signaling her that it was time to go. When she tried to thank Kdoma for everything he'd done for them, he said he'd simply tried to do his duty. There are higher rewards than human praise.

Ben was in surgery for most of the day. Karen had left the children in the care of an American family she'd met at the hotel. She paced the hall outside the operating theater, a long bleak hallway painted some terrible dark green color.

At least Jack and Jimmie were safe. Bless that village with its kind chief who took them in as if they were his family. Within two hours after the helicopter crashed, the federal army found them. They flew Karen and her boys to the capital, while Tom and Kelly left the country another way. It was hard for her to say good-bye to this couple who had helped them so much. They'd be returning to Mtobe as soon as the rebellion was defeated. Karen knew she never would.

While she paced in the hospital, she found it difficult to keep her thoughts from flitting everywhere. Her fear and anger and confusion drew her inward.

At long last the surgeon came out and told her that everything had gone well. She should go home and try to sleep. He was an African, with intelligence and good humor on his face, a man to be trusted.

The next morning she was back in the hospital at six. She didn't bring the children. It wasn't clear what Ben would look like or what his state of mind might be.

He was awake, with a weak smile lighting up his face. "Hi," he said, out of the contraptions and apparatus wrapped around him.

"Hi," she said back, sitting down on a chair near him and reaching out to take his hand.

"Don't worry," he said. "The doctor promised me I'd live."

"Kdoma pulled you into the church," she blurted. "He stopped the bleeding even though he'd been hurt too." She felt so awkward as she sat there and watched her strong husband suffer with the pain that stood clearly in his eyes.

"I don't remember much," he said. "Is Kdoma still alive?"

"He'll be fine."

"The kids?"

"Fine." She didn't tell him of her concern for Jack. There were too many burdens already in the room. "Harry Simpson called the embassy and left a message."

"What does my loyal boss have to say for himself?"

"Well, he insists that he really did try to find out where you were, but he couldn't locate you until after you'd been hurt."

"I have some things to say to him later," Ben said. "What about Saluso?"

"He was the one who shot you. He's dead, Ben."

"I'm sorry," he said, surprising her. "The captain?"

"He's dead too. Ben?" She paused. "I'm not sorry the governor's dead. Is that wrong of me?"

"Not if you didn't know him," he said. "Not if you just took the brunt of the stupid decisions he made."

"Why are you sorry he's dead then?" she asked.

"I guess because he finally convinced me that he did it for his country." Ben's voice had become very soft. "He was the perfect fanatic, so blinded by the rightness of his cause that he scarcely noticed how many people he had to trample to carry it out. Maybe if he'd really understood the faith he grew up in, he'd have taken another path. Who knows?"

"Are you saying he was justified in doing what he did to us?"

"No, Karen. He lost his right to be heard long ago. But he didn't do it for himself. That doesn't justify him, but maybe it helps explain him. I keep thinking how close I came to throwing God on the scrap heap just like he did."

"Why didn't you?"

"Because I couldn't make myself believe he wasn't there. You can't avoid him, and he's too big to throw away. You know, I've been thinking about something I read. Jacob, in the Bible, the man who wrestled with God. They fought all night. In the morning, God dislocated Jacob's hip because he wouldn't give up. Jacob never walked right again."

"No, Ben," she said.

"You know what's really amazing? I tried so hard to get Songo to surrender. I fought to save Kdoma from being hauled off to another country and tortured. Then, when everything came down, it didn't depend on me at all."

"Any one of us could have died, but we lived. You did your best, and we all prayed. And God..." Her voice trailed off, and Ben could see the tears welling in her eyes. She didn't think he could understand the turmoil in her heart. She didn't want to believe that she hated God. She wanted God to understand that she was grateful he'd saved their lives. But they could have been spared all this. He knew how much they'd suffered.

She stared at Ben, lying there so frail in his hospital bed, and he asked her, "Do they know yet whether I'll walk again?"

"The doctor is optimistic. But he says you'll always have a limp."

Ben unexpectedly smiled at that. There was a difference about him, a quietness, an acceptance.

"Jacob had a limp. God knows, he needed one," he said,

his voice so faint she could hardly hear him.

She didn't understand his meaning, so she just held his hand until he fell asleep.

It was fascinating the way his fingers clutched the cigarette, folding around it claw-like while it burned down to the filter. Harry Simpson. Chief of operations. He'd obviously forgotten how much the smoke irritated my lungs.

"Your last mission wasn't as satisfactory as OPSDEP had projected it to be," he said. Simpson always talked like that. OPSDEP was the Operations Department that made final decisions on virtually everything. Loosely translated, he was saying that Operations hadn't gotten the performance they wanted out of me. That, of course, made me the goat.

I watched him from the wrong side of his oversized desk, failing as usual to read any message at all in his face. The man lived beyond the rest of us common folks in a bureaucracy run by machines that were only pretending to be human so that consultants like me wouldn't be afraid of them. OPSDEP knew how to link names with assignments and send people to their fate. Beyond that there was no sign that rational thought came out of the committee room.

Since it didn't occur to me to be apologetic for blowing

my last sortie, I told him what was on my mind: "I'm sick of being hung out to dry by you people. Doesn't anybody do any research around here? First there was that knife in the arm two years ago from a guy who had murder on his mind. Then that Africa fiasco—"

"I've told you," Simpson said. "We had intelligence on the highest level with that one. Every indicator told us that Saluso wanted a free election."

"And you landed me in the middle of an attempted coup."

"Even if we'd given you all the data we had, you would have read it the same way we did. The only reason we didn't tell you more was that we were operating by need-to-know."

"Need-to-know" was always a handy excuse. If anyone needed to know, it was me because I was the guy with bullets flying past his head. Nobody ever told me much of anything.

"And I suppose this latest thing was my fault," I said.

"We were worried that your injury had put you off your form."

"The leg's getting better. It's been six months since they brought me home in a basket, so I was good and ready for this assignment."

"We gave you a simple scenario," he said. "Nothing covert. The president—"

"—dictator."

"—the president wanted nothing more than advice. He wasn't looking for anything beyond some basic training sessions. We gave the mission to you because it seemed easy enough for—"

"What? A gimp? A has-been?"

He ignored the self-pity. I was embarrassed because I usually managed to beat it down before it burst into speech.

"They took a dislike to you. The president, all of his advisors."

"I never talked to any advisors, and the whole thing was a fake from the beginning," I told him. "They needed a stamp of approval from someone in the West so they could show that it was going to be a clean election."

"It was."

"You saw my report. The president was scamming us, stacking the committee with his own people, probably doing dirty tricks on the other parties."

"I chose to interpret the circumstances more optimistically."

"People who have their heads in the clouds can't see where they're going."

"You're the one who abandoned the mission."

"Someone shot at me."

"Your side mirror broke. It could have been a rock."

"It wasn't a rock. Before I knew it, I'd been grabbed by a couple of sleeze-balls and almost eliminated."

"No one said they were under orders from the president. So you got roughed up by a pair of thieves. Our operatives are trained not to whine, Ben."

"Meaning what?"

"Meaning that you're losing your touch. There was a time when we could send you out and you always got the job done. Now we're having second thoughts about giving you overseas assignments. Maybe you'd be better working for us at home."

I stared at him, a hard-looking man with a face like a granite tombstone, the only concession to his humanity being his thinning hairline. Ex-marine captain, seemingly devoted to duty, but I didn't trust him anymore, and I wasn't surprised to hear him planning to offer me a desk job. I'd rattled his cage once too often, and it was time for him to rein me in.

"Does anyone ever have second thoughts about you, Harry?" I asked softly.

"Why should they?"

"Because you seem pretty accident prone." He bristled at that. "In fact, Harry, something smells, and I'm surprised the folks in the tower aren't holding their noses."

"Are you making an accusation, Ben?" he asked, his voice masking whatever he felt.

"Why? Do you want something slanderous for the tape recorder in your desk?"

He squirmed slightly, then said, "I just want to understand what it is that's led you to believe that I harbor desires to harm you."

"Almost two years ago, after taking a knife in the arm, my wife was kidnapped, and I learned that someone at Libertec was feeding information about my whereabouts to her captors. Then, just over six months ago, you sent me to Africa, right into the middle of a coup, and I caught a bullet that could have killed me."

"Ben," he said in a voice of reason, as if to silence my harangue. But I went on.

"Then you sent me to advise a Central American president who wants nothing to do with real democracy. All he's looking for is our stamp of approval on his scummy political agenda. Did you do any research, Harry? Have you done any research in the past two years?"

Surprisingly, he smiled. "I'm sure your job has been tense recently, Ben," he said. "The world is getting more complicated all the time, and I don't blame you for taking on some elements of paranoia considering what you've been through."

I resisted the urge to sneer and decided to find out where he was going. He went on:

"Actually, I have something completely different to offer you. Close to home, no risk."

"A desk job?"

"I thought you were sick of high adventure."

There was no point in pursuing it. If they wanted to put me out to pasture, I'd have to weigh my options.